W.E.B. DU BOIS

GRANDFATHER OF BLACK STUDIES

W.E.B. Du Bois

Nagueyalti Warren

AFRICA WORLD PRESS

Trenton | London | Cape Town | Nairobi | Addis Ababa | Asmara | Ibadan

AFRICA WORLD PRESS
541 West Ingham Avenue | Suite B
Trenton, New Jersey 08638

Copyright © 2011 Nagueyalti Warren
First Printing 2011

Book and cover design: Saverance Publishing Services

Library of Congress Cataloging-in-Publication Data

Warren, Nagueyalti.
  Grandfather of Black studies : W.E.B. Du Bois / Nagueyalti Warren.
    p. cm.
  Includes bibliographical references and index.
  ISBN 1-59221-822-9 (pbk.) -- ISBN 1-59221-821-0 (hardback)
  1. Du Bois, W. E. B. (William Edward Burghardt), 1868-1963--Juvenile literature. 2. African Americans--Biography--Juvenile literature. 3. African American intellectuals--Biography--Juvenile literature. 4. African American civil rights workers--Biography--Juvenile literature. 5. African Americans--Study and teaching (Higher)--History--20th century. 6. Blacks--Study and teaching (Higher)--History--20th century. I. Title.
  E185.97.D73W37 2011
  303.48'4092--dc22
  [B]
                                          2011002282

Dedicated to Frances E. Herrin
and the late Iris Anderson,
mother and grandmother, respectively

Table of Contents

FOREWORD

The writer's long intellectual acquaintance with the work of W.E.B. Du Bois from the writing of her dissertation over twenty years ago to the present is impressive. With this kind of historical engagement it is not surprising that this work is a most interesting account of Du Bois' contributions to Black or Africana Studies. Of particular import is the insight into Black Women's Studies, which is growing in prominence in the American academy. The perspective provided allows the reader to assess Du Bois' work in a different manner from that previously set forth by many writers. It sparks questions that will generate ideas for further research. For example, how have scholars of the modern 1960s movement that established the field in the academy expanded upon or been linked to Du Bois' ideas and plans for the systematic study of people of African descent in America and beyond? Will readers query the significance of Du Bois' work to the many volumes of work developed since the formal entry of a Black/Africana Studies in the academy? What attributes of Du Bois' work garners a prominence in the writings of contemporary scholars grounded in Black/Africana Studies? Significantly, chapters 1, 2, and 3 crystallize much of Du Bois' life and works that have been elaborated upon in other writings.

But more importantly, chapters 4 and 5 open discussion into areas that have received less attention than would be expected. This fresh approach is invigorating.

While the author in chapter 4, *A River of Knowledge*, examines the problems that have continually confronted Black/Africana Studies, she presents a splendid account of the charges against the field and presents a historical perspective of its struggle for recognition in higher education. The political struggle was particularly instructive, for no field in the academy has been subject to such deliberate and systematic attacks, which is but a microcosm of those faced by black people in America, as pointed out in *Out of the Revolution: The Development of Africana Studies*, edited by Delores P. Aldridge and Carlene Young in 2000. Chapter 4, *A River of Knowledge,* makes a gigantic leap to capture the philosophical and concrete contributions of Du Bois to Black Studies in the context of current curricula. Emphasis on these contributions to curriculum building is a significant accomplishment.

The last chapter, chapter 5, *His Deep and Abiding Love,* aptly addresses Du Bois' contribution to Black Women's Studies. The focus on Black Women's Studies is an important and necessary one, for it has garnered considerable discussion within the broader field of Africana/Black Studies and beyond. The author interrogates the subject matter in a provocative manner, revealing the various dimensions of gender issues. In fact, as I have written on several occasions over the last decade, attention to Black Women's Studies can not be minimized or marginalized if there is to be a full development of Africana/Black Studies or an understanding of American history. Importantly, no previous author has unveiled and analyzed so effectively Du Bois' perspective on women, beginning with significant women in his intimate domain and expanding to that of the broader realm of African American women and American society. As for the contribution of Du Bois to Africana/Black Studies in general and more specifically to Black Women Studies, Nagueyalti Warren provides an assessment that will be invaluable to those who would seek to grasp yet another insight into the mind and essence of this giant among scholars.

Chapter 5 is a fitting chapter to conclude this volume, for it points to what can be expected in the future as we study the lives and experiences of black people, with gender being a dynamic focus of any such discourse.

Delores P. Aldridge

Delores P. Aldridge, Ph.D., is the Grace Towns Hamilton Professor of Sociology and African American Studies at Emory University, the first distinguished chair named for an African American woman at a major institution.

ACKNOWLEDGEMENTS

I owe a debt of gratitude to many people who have enabled me to complete this book. I want especially to thank Dr. Robert A. Paul, Dean of Emory University College of Arts and Sciences, who graciously approved a year's sabbatical so that I could focus on the completion of this work. I wish to thank also my colleagues in the Department of African American Studies who covered for me while I was on leave, and to thank Dr. Mark Sanders in particular for his support in taking on added responsibilities. To the helpful librarians and staff at Fisk, Vanderbilt, Peabody, and Howard universities and at the Library of Congress, I say, "Thank you." Thanks also to Ali-Sha Dalton, my summer research assistant. My friends and colleagues, Dean Vera Dixon Rorie and Dr. Delores P. Aldridge, provided the good food, great shopping, and joyful laughter that I needed in order to return to my desk and work in solitary confinement.

To my family, I owe my gratitude for your love and devotion; and to my husband, my deepest appreciation for your constant understanding and support. To my children, who have watched my struggle and who hopefully have learned the meaning of sustained effort, I am indeed thankful for the encouragement your youthful optimism provides.

INTRODUCTION

This book began as my doctoral dissertation titled "The Contributions of W.E.B. Du Bois to Black Studies in Higher Education." Immediately upon receiving my degree, I became chairperson in the Department of English at Fisk University. Little did I know it would be more than twenty years before I could return to this research and revise it as a monograph. However, chairing a department, then working in administration as assistant and associate dean of Emory College consumed more time than I realized. Finally able to return to this project, I feared someone else would have captured my idea. Certainly many books have been written about Du Bois (pronounced Du Boys) since the 1980s. David Levering Lewis (1993, 2000) has written the definitive Du Bois biographies, and most recently Derrick P. Aldridge (2008) has examined Du Bois' educational philosophy. Manning Marable (1986) has looked closely at Du Bois' politics, and many others have reexamined the 1903 classic *The Souls of Black Folk*. However, none of these focused exclusively on the link between Du Bois' idea of Black Studies and what eventually entered the academy as the interdisciplinary field known by various names, from Black Studies, Afro-American Studies, African and African American Studies,

African American Studies, and finally to Africana Studies. James Stewart (1987) names Du Bois as the impetus for establishing a permanent base for Black Studies in institutions of higher education.

As evidenced in the literature surrounding the field, ambiguity exists as to the history, definition, and mission of Black Studies.[1] For instance, James Turner (1980) says Black Studies emerged as a field of study between 1930 and 1940. Others focus on the modern Black Studies movement of the 1960s and early 1970s (Asante 2007; Aldridge and Young 2000; Adams 1993; Clark Hine 1990). Fischer (1969) attributes the birth of Black Studies to the Civil Rights Movement, and even as late as 2009, the on-line U.S. History Encyclopedia defines Black Studies as developing in the late 1960s and 1970s. However, there is ample evidence that Black Studies has been around for a very long time in the scholarly works of a number of black people. Of these, the works of W.E.B. Du Bois and Carter G. Woodson generally are considered to have the greatest influence on shaping the roots of Black Studies.[2] Actually Du Bois was preeminent in setting the larger surrounding movement,[3] which incorporated the fields of history, literature, sociology, education, and the arts.

William Edward Burghardt Du Bois was a scholar, educator, historian, sociologist; an opponent and at times a supporter of Booker T. Washington, a prolific writer, Pan-Africanist, and fighter for black freedom and African liberation. The first empirical and sociological study of black Americans was conducted by Du Bois in 1896 when he collected data for his now classic work *The Philadelphia Negro*. As professor of history and economics at Atlanta University, Du Bois initiated the first program in higher education to study the black experience in America.

For a long time W.E.B. Du Bois' influence on the development of Black Studies was greatly underestimated.[4] During the heated debates of the late 1960s and 1970s, his name was seldom if ever mentioned. This omission led to many misconceptions regarding the discipline or field of study, as some insist is the appropriate nomenclature. Both monetary problems and issues of theory have beset Black Studies from the onset. Allen (1974) outlines the problems that plagued Black Studies in the following arguments:

1. Black Studies is political rather than academic, and therefore, has no place in higher education.
2. Black Studies is intellectually bankrupt; that is, it has no subject matter or theoretical base.
3. Black Studies has no standard curriculum.
4. Black Studies is a form of reverse racism.
5. A degree in Black Studies is not marketable.

In addition to these polemical assertions, a more fundamental question arose from the issue that if blacks indeed were Americans, why did they need separate study?

These questions, posed over forty years ago, still echo in the halls of the academy today. I teach the introductory course in African American Studies and face many of the same issues and challenges, not just from students but in the texts of black scholars. The debate on activism in Black Studies is crystallized in the argument between Henry Louis Gates, Jr., and Manning Marable.[5] Gates's "A Call to Protect Academic Integrity from Politics," is countered by Marable's "A Plea That Scholars Act upon, not Just Interpret, Events." [6]

Du Bois, in his various books and articles, answered the questions that continue to plague efforts to optimize the study of black people. And although his studies of black people were conducted long before the inception of the 1967–1970s controversy over the purpose and validity of Black Studies, Du Bois was acutely aware of these issues. In 1898, when he proposed conducting a scientific study of the black experience in America, he wrote that there would be opposition to his plans and anticipated that the objections would come from both white and black people. "The new study of the American Negro," Du Bois insisted, "must . . . from the outset [have] but one object, the ascertainment of the facts as to the social forces and conditions of one-eighth of the inhabitants of the land."[7] In spite of Du Bois' pioneering efforts, Black Studies, which is the systematic investigation and study of the black experience in America, did not find a place in the academy and within the curriculum of higher education until the student protests of the Black Power era.

Perhaps because Du Bois was an outspoken critic of American society and because many of his views were controversial, some academics have been reluctant to fully embrace and appreciate his contributions to American higher education. In 1983, when I presented my thesis proposal to a professor I hoped would chair my committee, he refused, stating that he had served in World War II and would not have anything to do with my study because Du Bois had been a Communist. I wonder if his response would have been the same had I proposed a study of Pablo Neruda's work.

Fortunately, today more of Du Bois' books are in print than there were twenty years ago, due in large part to the scholarship that continues to be produced about him. Philip Foner (1970) stated that until recently the contribution of W.E.B. Du Bois had been largely ignored. It is unfortunate that a black man who in 1895 penned the dissertation that became the first volume of the Harvard University Series in History would be ignored by scholars. The failure to recognize and document the contributions of Du Bois to the development of a philosophy and methodology for the scientific study of the black experience constitutes a problem and serious loss to the entire academic community. In particular, questions regarding the purpose of Black Studies and its validity in higher education Du Bois answered years before students brought their demands to the hallowed halls of learning. Indeed he could attack the questions and answer them so that they need never be questions again. Any remaining questions are not unanswered, rather the answers are suppressed, fragmented, or speciously disputed out of existence. With regard to the birth of Black Studies in the American academy, the questions that arose too often were an effort to stem the tide of student demands.

Du Bois' writings between 1896 and 1910 are significant to the development and philosophy of Black Studies. Of course his education and life experiences helped to formulate his ideas and in some ways presented a paradox in terms of cultural identity—producing what he called "double consciousness." Du Bois not only laid the groundwork for the study of black Americans, but he set forth remarkably clear academic standards. Thus, this study scrutinizes Du Bois' concept of the purpose and design of Black Studies in higher education. Du Bois' contributions to the struggle for civil rights and racial equality are well documented. His contribution to Black Studies in particular is one of the few areas awaiting more analysis. The information and ideas detailed in his works could influence the direction and policies of future Black Studies programs.

Du Bois himself never used the idiom *Black Studies.* In the period of United States history during which he researched, the nomenclature for black Americans was *negro* with a small n. Thus, Black Studies is new terminology. In the field itself the term is somewhat dated. What began as Black Studies became Afro-American Studies, African and African American Studies, and is still evolving into Africana Studies and in some places developing as Diaspora Studies. I have chosen to use the original terminology for several reasons. First, I want to honor Du Bois' black consciousness for using the word *black* when it was most detested by black people themselves as well as in American society. The title of his 1903 classic, *The Souls of Black Folk*, juxtaposed souls, that which is spiritual and divine to that which was thought of as unworthy. The effect was profound. Second, the use of Black Studies honors those who struggled to establish it in academies across the nation and contextualizes the period in which it took place.

In 1906 Du Bois defined his plan as the "systematic and exhaustive study of the American Negro." [8] This study examines his work in light of the programs and ideas that exist today regarding Black Studies in higher education.

Chapter 1, The Boy is Father of the Man, examines Du Bois' childhood in light of the social and political atmosphere of his day. His educational, professional, and political experiences are also analyzed. Basic information for this chapter was mainly derived from Du Bois' autobiographies, from other autobiographical writings, and from biographies, one in particular written by his second wife, Shirley G. Du Bois. Also, the Lewis biography as well as conversations with Du Bois' stepson (Shirley Graham Du

Bois' son), David Graham Du Bois, comprise the basis for this analysis.

Chapter 2, A Talented Tenth, examines the formulation of Du Bois' educational and political philosophy and analyzes the issues that arose between Du Bois and Booker T. Washington.

Chapter 3, The Soul of Du Bois, discusses the intellectual contributions of Du Bois to Black Studies, beginning with the Department of Labor Reports. *The Philadelphia Negro* and the Atlanta University Studies are also examined. The chapter ends with an analysis of Du Bois' other writings that contribute to the philosophical foundation of Black Studies and includes an annotated bibliography of Du Bois' published and unpublished works, which contribute to the subject matter of Black Studies.

Chapter 4, A River of Knowledge, examines the problems that have continually confronted Black Studies. It also outlines the various charges against Black Studies and presents an historical perspective of its struggle for recognition in higher education. This chapter links the philosophical and concrete contributions of Du Bois to Black Studies in the context of current curricula and includes an annotated bibliography of his works.

Chapter 5, His Deep and Abiding Love, examines Du Bois' contribution to Black Women's Studies and summarizes and concludes the study.

CHAPTER 1

THE BOY IS FATHER OF THE MAN

He began to have a dim feeling, that to attain his place in the world, he must be himself and not another.

—Of Our Spiritual Strivings Du Bois 1903

"Unto you a child is born," Du Bois wrote in "Of the Passing of the First-Born"[1] as he marveled at the miracle of childbirth. His son was born in the Berkshire Hills of Massachusetts, just as Du Bois had been some twenty-nine years earlier. Du Bois was the second son born to Mary Silvina Burghardt Du Bois. Adelbert Burghardt, born in 1862, according to David Levering Lewis, Du Bois' biographer, is the half-brother Du Bois names only briefly in his autobiography. Six years his senior, it is not known to what extent Du Bois interacted with his brother. What is clear from Du Bois' writings is that he bonded completely with his New England environment. He describes his birthplace in great detail. Great Barrington is located twenty-eight miles from the Hudson River, bounded on the south by Connecticut and on the west by New York.[2] South of Main Street on Route 23 at the edge of town is the tract of land where Du Bois was born. The house where he lived is no longer standing; however, in 1969 the site was proclaimed a national memorial.[3]

William Edward Burghardt Du Bois was born in a leap year, February 23, 1868, on a Sunday. He descended on his mother's side from the "black Burghardts" who were, according to him, "a group of African Negroes descended from Tom, who was born in West Africa about 1730."[4] Tom had been abducted by Dutch slave traders and brought to New England as a child. He served in the Revolutionary War and eventually freed himself from slavery. The Burghardts (the name was taken from a white family of Dutch descent for whom Tom worked) settled in Massachusetts where they remained for almost 200 years.[5]

Less is known about Du Bois' paternal ancestry, and since the Lewis biography was published there is a lot to question. His grandfather descended from a black Bahamian woman and a French Huguenot father. The grandfather married a black Haitian woman; and their son, Alfred Du Bois, was W.E.B. Du Bois' father (Du Bois 1968). Alfred Du Bois married Mary Burghardt; however, the Burghardt family disapproved of the union, and soon after Du Bois was born, his father left Great Barrington, never to be seen or heard from again. According to Lewis, Alfred was probably a bigamist, certainly was a Civil War deserter, and he definitely neglected and deserted his son. Instead of blaming these shortcomings on the man he never knew, Du Bois invented a father, one he imagined as a natural "dreamer—romantic, indolent, kind, unreliable[,]," one who had the makings of a poet or adventurer. [6]

Du Bois was raised by a single parent and her extended family, in which at least one child's and perhaps even his own legitimacy was questioned. This so-called broken home, a term used until recently to describe families where the parents were either separated or divorced, flew in the face of the Victorian concepts of domestic virtue and the importance placed upon the legitimacy of one's offspring. Although Du Bois in the *Autobiography* (1968) claims that they lived on the "edge of poverty,"[7] Lewis describes that edge of poverty on Railroad Street as "two blocks of perdition, a foul causeway of ruin through three or four saloons, gambling dens, and at least one house of prostitution."[8] Du Bois' background, which he apparently attempted to ameliorate in his three autobiographies, is similar to the lives of many black children today and makes his contributions and achievements all the more profound. He was not a New England blueblood; nor was he a descendant from college-educated parents, but rather was a first-generation college student. Considering that Du Bois was born only three years after slavery ended (1865), one might erroneously conclude that all blacks would be first-generation college educated. Such was not the case, particularly in the North. There was in fact perhaps not a talented tenth, but certainly a talented percentage of the black population that were formally educated, degree-holding citizens.

George B. Vashon graduated from Oberlin College in 1844 with a bachelor of arts degree and later earned a master's. He became the third black person to hold a teaching post in a white college or university. From 1854 until 1857 he was professor of literature and mathematics at New York Central College.[9] In 1849 both Charles

L. Reason and William Allen were professors at the same college.[10] Black people attended Oberlin as early as 1835, just two years after it opened.[11] Nine years before Du Bois was born, Wilberforce opened its doors, and by 1858 student enrollment reached 200. The first black woman college instructor, Sarah Jane Woodson Early, taught literature at Wilberforce in 1858. She received her education at Oberlin, graduating in 1856.[12] Du Bois, therefore, was not as privileged as he might have appeared prior to the publication of the Lewis biography.

When compared to Booker T. Washington some scholars[13] have pointed out that Du Bois' life experiences growing up in New England were far different from Washington's in the South. While it is true that Du Bois was never enslaved, nor did he as a child witness the rabid activities of the Ku Klux Klan, nevertheless, similarities can be drawn between him and Washington. Both were of mixed racial heritage, both grew up fatherless, reared by a single mother whom they helped to support; and both saw education as a way to improve their lot and that of other black people. As adolescents both were greatly impressed by the manners and mores of Victorian society: Du Bois by observing his grandfather and Washington by his association with the New England teachers and Samuel Armstrong at Hampton Institute. Both, in fact, were self-invented, self-made men.

Du Bois' mother suffered a paralytic stroke from which she never fully recovered when Du Bois was about seven years old. In spite of her disability, she insisted that he continue attending school regularly. At the age of six Du Bois began attending Great Barrington's public schools and went regularly from nine a.m. until four p.m., five days a week, ten months a year. He excelled in his studies and advanced rapidly, so that he completed high school at age sixteen. In 1884 he graduated, the only black student in a class of thirteen.[14]

Du Bois' ancestry, his physical, sociopolitical environment, and his childhood experiences, all doubtlessly contributed to the man W.E.B. Du Bois became. Yet his childhood experiences are not quite what one might have expected from so militant a social critic and advocate for social justice. Of his childhood he wrote:

> I had, as a child, almost no experience of segregation or color discrimination. My schoolmates were invariably white; I knew nevertheless that I was exceptional in appearance and that this riveted attention upon me. Less clearly, I early realized that most of the colored persons I saw, including my own folk, were poorer than the well-to-do whites; lived in humbler houses, and did not own stores.[15]

Yet Great Barrington was not too unusual in its apparent disregard of color. Otherwise his mother would not have armed him with her belief about discrimination. She told him that "the secret of life and the loosing of the color bar, then, lay in excellence in accomplishment. . . . There was no real discrimination on account of color—it was all a matter of ability and hard work."[16] Thus, Du Bois, as an adolescent, assumed that success was contingent on one's own efforts, and that the poor and unsuccessful were themselves blameworthy.[17] Leslie Lacy observes that Du Bois was, as a young boy, a perfect product of his environment.[18] Du Bois himself stated, "Had it not been for the race problem, I should have probably been an unquestioning worshipper at the shrine of the social order and economic development into which I was born."[19] Indeed, Du Bois for many years was a Europhile.

The larger social setting in which Du Bois grew up is partially described in the *Autobiography* when he writes about the Japanese emperors' rise to power, the Chinese Empress Dowager's fight for power, the opening of the Suez Canal, Germany, Great Britain, and Africa. Du Bois as a world citizen understood the butterfly effect. A wing flutter in the West could cause a tsunami in the East. The Meiji emperors to whom Du Bois refers were the family of Emperor Mutsuhito (Meiji), who came to power in 1867. This historical period lasted until 1912, when Emperor Yoshihito ascended the throne, marking the beginning of the Taisho period. The Meiji period was significant because it marked the beginning of the modern state of Japan. The leaders of this period were concerned with foreign policy and acutely aware of the imperialist activities of the West, particularly in Africa and in Asia.[20] These political developments were of interest to Du Bois, who would one day attack imperialism in all its various forms.

China underwent changes similar to those that took place in Japan as China began to develop a vague socialism. Both China in particular and socialism in general would have a great impact on Du Bois' life and philosophy. The events of 1871 in Germany were prelude to one of the most racist powers in the West, a power that multiplied until the collapse of the Third Reich in 1945.[21] Germany also has significance in that Du Bois was to spend part of his life studying there.

Benjamin Disraeli's significance to Du Bois lies in the fact that as prime minister of Great Britain, Disraeli's leadership produced many social reforms such as slum clearance, a public health act, factory legislation, and laws on trade unions. Disraeli's leadership therefore exhibited the kind of social commitment Du Bois would spend his life advocating for in the United States.

In 1868 Ethiopia (known as Abyssinia) was invaded by British troops. War ensued, and there were many years of repeated invasions by European forces. In 1896 the Ethiopians defeated the invading Italians and were recognized as an independent country. The victory of Ethiopia foreshadowed the future liberation of colonial Africa. Du Bois, with his love of Africa, would spearhead the fight against colonialism.

Finally, the opening of the Suez Canal in 1869 had a momentous effect on the economic balance of the world in which Du Bois was to live for ninety-five years. The politics of the canal symbolized for Du Bois many aspects of imperialist exploitation.[22] In the years before Du Bois was born, the United States struggled with questions regarding slavery. In 1863 the Dred Scott decision was annulled, and it was declared that "Free men of color, if born in the United States, are citizens of the United States."[23] On January 1, 1863, the Emancipation Proclamation became official. The great freedom fighters—Frederick Douglass, Sojourner Truth, and Harriet Tubman—had fought and won, at least technically. In 1866 Fisk University opened its doors, an event that would significantly impact Du Bois' education. The year of his birth the government ratified the Fourteenth Amendment, which established the concept of "equal protection" for all citizens under the laws of the Constitution; and ex-slave Oscar J. Dunn became lieutenant governor of Louisiana.[24]

During the time that Du Bois was attending the white schools of Great Barrington, black people in the South were faced with a series of "Black Codes," which were attempts by the southern states to reinstate white control over the lives of the newly freed black people.[25] During Reconstruction the Ku Klux Klan provided extralegal sanctions for maintaining white supremacy. Beginning in 1873 the United States Supreme Court destroyed many of the protections that congressional legislation had established during Reconstruction. In the Slaughter-House Case (1873), the Court ruled that the Fourteenth Amendment's privileges and immunities referred only to the inherent characteristics of United States citizenship.[26] In the *United States v Cruickshank* (1876), the Court shifted to the states the right and responsibility for guaranteeing blacks the right to vote; and then in the *United States v Reese* (1876), the Court ruled that the Fifteenth Amendment did not confer the right to vote. Furthermore, according to Bergman, the Court stated that "sections 3 & 4 of the Enforcement Act of the Fifteenth Amendment of May 31, 1870, were unconstitutional."[27] By 1875 a so-called New South was born, and white northern and federal support for black people had all but disappeared. The United States Supreme Court, in 1883, declared that the Civil Rights Act of 1875 was unconstitutional.[28] The South was left to work out its own racial problem, and this was the South that Du Bois would enter, a South where he would witness lynchings, night raids, terror, and death for black families; yet, it was also a place where he would find his true identity, crystallize his dreams, and set his lifelong goals.

Who was the boy that became the man W.E.B.? Lewis, in the biography, introduces Willie, a lefty with a brilliant mind, great ambition, and a desire for knowledge. Willie was reared as an only child for the most part. He benefited from his mother's undivided attention. His one visit to his paternal grandfather greatly impressed the adolescent with what today might be perceived as superfluous manners. The boy Willie grew up in the Victorian era and valued what was thought of as good breeding. The man that Willie became epitomized the pride and manliness he glimpsed in grandfather Du Bois. Thus, Willie became the gentleman with the top hat and cane. Part of his formality may have come from his physical stature. Were it not for his biographer's detailed research, few would have guessed that the boy who became W.E.B. Du Bois was just 5 feet 5 inches tall, for he created a towering persona.

As a result of the Civil War the economic climate of Du Bois' time was especially complicated. Inflation caused banks to become insolvent, businesses to fail, and factories to close. Agriculture was severely crippled in the South with the loss of slave labor. Yet, the economy in the North was such that it could boast of approximately three-fourths of the nation's wealth. The North excelled in manufacturing, shipping, and banking. For a time, cotton was king in the South. Several historians suggest that the South was depending on the economic importance of cotton to help them win the war. The textile factories of England were also heavily dependent on southern cotton. But "king wheat and king corn—both Northern agricultural royalty—proved to be more potent potentates than king cotton."[29] The North was able to supply the British with the wheat and corn that they needed more than cotton.

Thus, the North economically fared far better than the South because the former had a disproportionate share of the wealth. During the Civil War period income taxes were first levied in the North. This tax produced millions of dollars. Green-backed paper money also was issued. Between 1861 and 1865 the North collected a total of $667,163,247 in taxes.[30] The National Banking System, authorized by Congress in 1863, was a financial landmark. Banks grew throughout the North at a swift rate. The beginning of the war had produced an economic depression, but as the fighting continued industry boomed; new factories opened under the shelter of new protective tariffs. The Civil War, ironically, gave birth to the first millionaire class in the history of the United States.[31]

Thus, Du Bois was born into an economic era that marked an end to the agrarian slaveocracy of the South and a beginning of the industrial plutocracy of the North. Du Bois was born into one of the wealthiest states in the union. Yet, having been born black, this state's wealth may have had little direct effect upon him. Nevertheless, he did benefit from his state's educational system of public schools, and one can speculate that had he been born into the war-ravaged South his life would have been vastly different. While Massachusetts could boast of cities like Boston with teeming seaports and wealthy citizens, Du Bois described the economic life of Great Barrington as middle class, working class, and a few with inherited wealth. He claimed that the contrast between the haves and the have nots was not great.[32]

Although it has not been fully established just how and to what extent social and environmental factors affect human growth and development, one can say that Du Bois' early environment, the social and political atmosphere of the United States, and the world, as well as the economic conditions of his time must surely have been contributing factors to the way he came to view the world.

After high school Du Bois wanted most to attend Harvard College because he said it was the oldest and the best; however, he was discouraged from this pursuit. Family and friends advised that he was too young, sixteen, to go directly to college, suggesting instead that he work and study for a year and then enter college in the fall of 1885.[33] However, in the fall of 1884, according to the *Autobiography*, his mother died. Apparently Du Bois' memory failed him as he mentioned it might have, writing about an event that had occurred more than sixty years prior. Mary Silvina actually did not die until March 1885.[34] As an orphan, Du Bois was penniless. The town of Great Barrington, aware of his intellectual ability, banded together and provided a scholarship for Du Bois to attend Fisk University in Nashville, Tennessee.[35] Despite the protest of his extended family (aunts, uncles, cousins), who resented the idea of him being sent to the South, Du Bois welcomed the opportunity to escape the "spiritual isolation" that surrounded him in New England.[36] One wonders if this too is not something that he might have felt in retrospect. He claims he wanted to join the members of his own race and age, for the number of black people in Great Barrington numbered no more than fifty in a population of 5,000.[37] Whether or not this longing for racial association was true at the time or whether, looking back over his life Du Bois remembers what he perhaps thought he should have felt, is open to question.

What is certain is that going south marked a significant turning point in Du Bois' life. He described his trip as going to a world ". . . split into white and black halves . . . where the darker half was held back by race prejudice and legal bonds, as well as by deep ignorance and dire poverty."[38] Henceforth, his mother's naive explanation and/or the New England work ethic would not be able to explain away inequality in American society. The trip to the South was his first encounter with and acknowledgment of racism. Du Bois would later come to realize just how much sheer luck played in his becoming Dr. Du Bois. In the last *Autobiography* he muses over the fact that his mother might have preferred that he work instead of attend school; or once caught for stealing fruit, he might have been remanded to reform school, something that the Great Barrington judge had considered doing.[39] What if the principal at his high school had discouraged rather than encouraged him? His life might then have been like Malcolm X's, who years later would be told by a teacher that black people could not become lawyers. The journey south also illustrates an inward journey that Du Bois took toward self-identity. Of the unfortunate situation he found in the South, Du Bois wrote: "But facing this was not a lost group, but at Fisk a microcosm of a world and a civilization in potentiality. Into this world I leapt with enthusiasm. A new loyalty and allegiance replaced my Americanism: henceforth I was a Negro."[40] Probably Fisk did much to enable Du Bois in the process of inventing himself. His newly found identity was suffused with racial pride and flourished in the black college environment. His feelings were expressed most clearly in the *Autobiography* when he marveled at the intelligence exhibited in the black youth of a race only twenty years removed from slavery.[41]

At Fisk Du Bois found himself in the company of older and more mature students who had experienced the violence of Reconstruction in the South. The faculty at Fisk consisted of white northerners. Therefore, Du Bois' cultural background "suffered no change or hiatus,"[42] as his schooling previously had been by white instructors only. Academically, Du Bois was ahead of his peers who had not been privileged to attend elementary and secondary schools regularly, and who, in the "colored public schools" of the South, had not been adequately prepared for the rigors of college. He completed Fisk University in three years, graduating in a class of five with a bachelor of arts degree on June 13, 1888, at 10 a.m.[43]

Du Bois had gone to the South and claimed his heritage, found his identity, formulated his life plans, and had begun to develop his *Weltanschauung*. Of the Fisk experience he concluded that "the excellent and earnest teaching, the small college classes, the absence of distractions, either in athletics or society,"[44] enabled him to understand his life mission, which was to work for the true freedom and progress of black people. He says he replaced an "egocentric world" of rugged individualism with "a world centering and whirling about . . . race in America."[45] This he certainly did do, but as with most things regarding motivating factors, the situation is more complicated than the way Du Bois presents his dawning racial commitment. Lewis discerns that Du Bois' "feelings about race in these early years were more labile or tangled, not to say conflicted, than his public professions revealed."[46] Lewis concludes that because of Du Bois' mixed heritage, he was actually ambivalent about race. But even this ambivalence he used to serve himself and to provide a "resilient superiority complex."[47]

The education and the creation of the man who became Dr. W.E.B. Du Bois did not only take place on the Fisk campus. During the summers he taught in the country schools of rural Tennessee. There, in the backwoods of Tennessee he acquired education, political awareness and social consciousness, and even sexual awareness that until his college years had been missing from his experience. He recalls that between 1885 and 1894, 1,700 black people were lynched. Each death marred his soul.[48] These murders, the maiming, the raping of black women, the Klan terrorism and destruction of lives and property impacted Du Bois as a young man and propelled him toward the conclusion that he articulated in 1900 at the First Pan-African Conference in London. In his address "To the Nations of the World," Du Bois declared, "the problem of the 20th century is the problem of the color line."[49]

In the fall of 1888, Du Bois finally realized his goal of attending Harvard College. He was admitted as a junior, despite possessing his undergraduate degree from Fisk. Du Bois came to Harvard, as he describes himself, a mature student seeking to enlarge his "grasp of the meaning of the universe."[50] He came there uninterested in fraternities and social life, which might not have been the case had he entered Harvard directly from high school. Had he gone directly from high school he believed he would have sought companionship with the white fellows and been disappointed and embittered by a discovery of social limitations to which he had not been accustomed. But he came by way of Fisk and the South, and there he had accepted color caste and embraced the companionship of his own race.[51] At Harvard, Du Bois found what he had hoped for; better books, better laboratories, and other academic enhancements that Fisk's endowment could not afford. However, he did not find better teachers "but teachers better known, who had wider facilities for gaining knowledge and had a broader atmosphere for approaching truth."[52]

Du Bois studied chemistry, geology, social science, philosophy, and history. At Harvard he also approached what was later to become sociology. In June 1890, he graduated cum laude with a bachelor of arts degree in Philosophy. He was one of six commencement speakers out of his class of 300.[53] His address, "Jefferson Davis: Representative of Civilization," received national attention, although much of its subtle irony and biting sarcasm was lost on his listeners, who praised him for his generous treatment of Davis and marveled at the fact that he was a black man. In the speech Du Bois indicts not only the United States but Western civilization for "moral obtuseness." His speech also exhibits the development of his own social consciousness—the consciousness of one who once had all but worshipped at the altar of Western civilization. The commencement speech given at Harvard reflects his shift, as Du Bois presents a scathing characterization of the confederate leader ". . . Jefferson Davis: now advancing civilization by murdering Indians, now hero of a national disgrace, called by courtesy the Mexican War; and finally as the crowning absurdity, the peculiar champion of a people fighting to be free in order that another people should not be free."[54] Juxtaposed the Davis speech was his Fisk address on "Bismarck" as hero, who actually was a supreme imperialist and convener of the conference that divided Africa into European colonies. Both speeches demonstrate his growth. Du Bois later explained that his choice of Bismarck "showed the abyss between my education and the truth."[55] The Harvard address foreshadows Du Bois' final condemnation and rejection of a society that could not or would not rid itself of bigotry.

At age twenty-two Du Bois did not think his formal education was complete. Despite almost continuous school attendance from age six, he had only just begun his training in the knowledge of social conditions and had merely begun taking his first steps toward the study of sociology. He defined sociology as "the science of human action,"[56] to be approached through a detailed study of history. Therefore, Du Bois remained at Harvard, and in 1892 he was awarded the master of arts degree in History.

Later that year he was elected to the American Historical Society.

Du Bois' quest for knowledge continued after he received his master's degree. He therefore decided he needed to study abroad. Manning Marable suggests that Du Bois probably decided to study abroad while still a student at Fisk.[57] The natural choice was Germany, for German universities at that time were famous for their graduate schools. Du Bois applied for a Slater Fund Fellowship to study in Germany at the University of Berlin, after sending a blistering letter to Rutherford B. Hayes, former U.S. president and chairman of the Slater Fund. His letter outlined the prejudice against assisting blacks in obtaining a truly liberal education. Subsequently he was awarded the fellowship.[58] At the same time he was also accepted as a candidate for a Ph.D. degree at Harvard.

Du Bois spent two years in Europe, an experience that broadened his perspective, although it did not temper his racial commitment. He was rapidly becoming a nonconformist. Others of his training were content, or seemingly so, with the current social order and trends. His own explanation was that racism and cultural contacts were so problematic they forced either protest or denial.[59] He chose to be among the protesters. As his formal education advanced, his interests became more concentrated on race. Du Bois realized, however, that to focus on one thing exclusively was to neglect others. He admits that his focus was narrow and explains "[What I] was trying to conceive and study, related themselves primarily to the plight of the comparatively small group of American Negroes with which I was identified, and theoretically to the larger Negro race. I did not face the general plight and conditions of all humankind."[60] The academy rewards as specialization the kind of focus Du Bois described.

Ironically, perhaps, Du Bois' European experience in a sense made him more of a humanitarian. In the *Autobiography* he says he "was not less fanatically a Negro, but 'Negro' meant a greater, broader sense of humanity and world fellowship."[61] He believed that "color prejudice" was limited to America's "narrowness."[62] In Germany he discovered how to view the world as a man unhampered by a racial and provincial outlook. It was there that Du Bois began to formulate his political and economical theory of slavery and racism.[63] Du Bois' formal classroom education ended when he was twenty-six years old.

In 1894 he returned to the United States from Germany. Two years later he produced his dissertation entitled, "The Suppression of the African Slave Trade to the United States of America, 1638–1870" for which he was awarded the Doctor of Philosophy degree from Harvard, making him the first black person to receive this terminal degree in the university's two-hundred-plus-year-old history. Thus ended Du Bois' college and university training. He now thought himself capable of achieving his life's goal: the liberation of black people.

CHAPTER 2

A TALENTED TENTH

To stimulate wildly weak and untrained minds
is to play with mighty fires.

—*Of the Training of Black Men* 1903

That Du Bois was talented is unquestionable. The young, highly educated Du Bois placed a tremendous amount of confidence in other Black people who like himself were well-educated, socially conscious citizens inclined to help change the racist nature of the United States. What he failed to anticipate was the extent to which capitalist materialism would work to undo a sense of collective identity among his black colleagues. The idea itself of a talented class lifting up the masses smacks of elitism; and yet it is easy to understand how the inexperienced Du Bois would embrace wholeheartedly the idea of noblesse oblige.

The idea that Du Bois began to process while he was still a graduate student or perhaps even earlier while he was a student at Fisk, the talented tenth, was for a race recently emancipated from slavery. Du Bois' idea articulated in his *Autobiography* was to provide a liberal arts education to "a Talented Tenth who through their knowledge of modern culture could guide the American Negro into a higher civilization."[1] He goes on to say that unless black leadership is forthcoming, the race will be forced to accept white leaders who could not be trusted to "guide this group into self-realization and to its highest cultural possibilities."[2] Du Bois' idea unwittingly led to the formation of a black "intelligentsia," many of whom were unwilling or unable to fight for justice for the black masses.

The problem with the talented tenth was that they were too much a part of the so-called higher civilization to which Du Bois referred. While segregated from social interactions with whites, the values and esthetics of the talented tenth were nonetheless being formulated in a white Western context. Du Bois' view is Eurocentric, a term not current in his day. Nevertheless, the standard by which culture was measured was that of modern Europe. Describing the talented tenth he wrote:

> There are in this land a million men of Negro blood, well-educated, owners of homes, against the honor of whose womanhood no breath was ever raised, whose men occupy positions of trust and usefulness and who, judged by any standard, have reached the full measure of the best type of modern European culture.[3]

Du Bois insisted that it is not fair to "belittle" their aspirations. Charging this "aristocracy of talent and character"[4] with raising the masses of black people, he asserted that always "culture" filters from the top downward.

Herein lies an assumption that was generally accepted until challenged by Langston Hughes and other young writers in the Harlem Renaissance, who saw the black masses as the repository of authentic black culture. The idea was embraced and enlarged upon during the Black Arts Movement. An identity crisis lies at the heart of Du Bois' belief that average ordinary folk needed to be pulled up to the level of European culture. On the one hand, he never defined exactly what culture meant to him. We can surmise that it includes the arts, but he might also mean that the masses of black people needed to be pulled up from ignorance to knowing. Still one wonders exactly what were they to know, the libretto of an opera or the lyrics of the Blues, the music of Brahms or ragtime?

Still another problem with Du Bois' philosophy concerning culture is the distinction between European and American. In his personal life we see the choices that he made in sending his only surviving child to a British boarding school. Clearly he favored European culture, but even this point must be qualified, for he believed that Europe was less racist than the United States. Bernard Bell observes that Du Bois' dilemma results from his cultural elitism that is in tension with his appreciation and use of black folk art.[5] James Baldwin more than a quarter century later, suffers a similar identity predicament. In "Stranger in the Village," finding himself the lone black person in a Swiss village, he wrote:

> For this village, even were it incomparably more remote and incredibly more primitive, is the West, the West onto which I have been so strangely grafted. These people cannot be, from the point of view of power, strangers anywhere in the world; they have made the modern world.

.. even if they do not know it. The most illiterate among them is related, in a way that I am not, to Dante, Shakespeare, Michelangelo, Aeschylus, Di Vinci, Rembrandt, and Racine; the cathedral at Chartres says something to them which it cannot say to me, as indeed would New York's Empire State Building, should anyone here ever see it. Out of their hymns and dances come Beethoven and Bach. Go back a few centuries and they are in their full glory—but I am in Africa, watching the conquerors arrive.[6]

When Du Bois employed the word *civilization*[7] it implied that the black masses are uncivilized. It also calls black character into question when he says education "must strengthen the Negro's character. . . ."[8] Furthermore, he makes an argument against trade schools insisting "that alone will not civilize a race of ex-slaves." He defines education as "a whole system of human training within and without the school house walls," thereby enforcing the point that training refers to "a heritage of bad habits"[9] that beset the newly freed. Perhaps the habits to which he refers included a disinclination to work, having been forced to do so without compensation, or the habit of stealing food, lying, or other habits of passive resistance and survival. Education for the formerly enslaved was to be training in morals and manners. Ironically, this morals and manners philosophy of education would prevail in historically black colleges and universities until the revolutionary nineteen sixties when the students demanded change.[10]

The talented tenth by virtue of their background (sons and daughters of free blacks or mixed race children educated in the North), apparently had both the manners and morals needed to become leaders. However, historian

Eugene Provenzo, Jr., argues that Du Bois' idea for this elite group had no chance of succeeding until the Civil Rights Movement of the 1960s. Provenzo does not say why the plan would not work, and Du Bois had research on his side that showed 50 percent of northern-born college men came to the South to work among the masses and 90 percent of southern-born graduates worked among the black people in the South.[11] The talented tenth always existed even in the direst of circumstances, thus Du Bois argues convincingly that leadership should begin at the top and not the bottom. Provenzo, Jr., correctly observes, however, that "while [Du Bois] objected to white domination of black people, he [did] not seem to have considered the possibility that a black elite or Talented Tenth could have their own class and social biases that did not necessarily conform with the needs and interests of the black masses."[12] While it is true that in 1903 Du Bois had a blind spot regarding class prejudice, he did not remain forever unaware.

By 1948, when he delivered the "Talented Tenth: Memorial Address" at Wilberforce, Du Bois indeed recognized the problems within his youthful philosophy. He told the surprised elite that leadership required "sacrifice . . . and [a] just distribution of wealth."[13] He proposed a "Guiding Hundredth" and said that talent simply was not enough to qualify one for black leadership. Talent, he learned, did not necessarily produce a social consciousness or a willingness to sacrifice for the good of the group. However, he might never have escaped his own personal ideal of elitism, as Provenzo suggests, because Du Bois continued to detest what he referred to as the "Blind worshippers of the average"[14]; as well there are numerous stories about his arrogance. Literary critic J. Saunders Redding, in a "Portrait" of Du Bois, says that people respected him for his accomplishments but saw him as "a crusty, mordant-witted snob of both the intellectual and social varieties."[15] While his personality may have suffered from the imitations of Victorian mores, his intellect did not. He was always thinking how to improve the United States and the world.

Frederick Douglass's death in 1895, Sojourner Truth's in 1883, and Henry Highland Garnet's in 1882, left Booker T. Washington the leading figure in black politics and education. His fame spread throughout the Diaspora and to Africa. Initially unopposed in his plans to improve the conditions of blacks, Washington had a free hand in organizing higher education in the so-called New South. When Du Bois started his professional career in 1894, he was employed to teach Greek and Latin at Wilberforce University in Ohio. Had the letter from Washington inviting him to teach in Alabama reached Du Bois before he accepted the offer from Wilberforce, he would have gone to Tuskegee. One can only wonder how things might have developed had Du Bois become a member of the Tuskegee machine.

Nevertheless, in the beginning of Du Bois' career he was not opposed to Washington's philosophy of black education; and even later when his opposition to Washington was clear, he continued to insist that both liberal arts and industrial arts were needed. Interestingly, Hampton Institute, the model for Tuskegee, was not initially focused on trade and industrial training but was a normal school that supplied teachers. Historian James Anderson points out that the Hampton-Tuskegee curriculum did not center on trade or agricultural training. More than twenty years after Hampton was founded, the first trade certificates were awarded. In 1900, only 45 of the 656 students enrolled at Hampton were in the trade school division, and only four students majored in agriculture.[16] However, by the time Du Bois entered the educational arena, the push clearly was for the "education" of black people that would not challenge white hegemony.

At Wilberforce, Du Bois tried to introduce a course in sociology, but the university would have no part of it. His experience at Wilberforce foreshadows the resistance he was to encounter throughout his long and varied career. Unable to realize his professional goals at Wilberforce, Du Bois left in 1896. While he was prevented from implementing any of his "new fangled" ideas at Wilberforce, it was there that he began to formulate his plan for a program of Black Studies (Du Bois 1968). Du Bois had determined that he would emancipate black people, and that history and the social sciences would be his weapons, augmented by "applied research and writing."[17] With this plan in mind, Du Bois accepted a temporary appointment of one year at the University of Pennsylvania as assistant instructor of sociology.[18]

The University of Pennsylvania gave him no official academic rank, no office space, no contact with students, very little contact with faculty; and he reported in the *Autobiography* that his name was eventually omitted from the catalogue.[19] In spite of mistreatment in this city of brotherly love, he set about to study the black people in Philadelphia. His research became the first scientific study on black people in the United States.[20] This study was extremely important in Du Bois' professional growth as well as in the development of his philosophy. He believed the problem of Blacks in the United States was a matter for "systematic investigation and intelligent understanding.

The world was thinking wrong about race," he asserted, "because it did not know. The ultimate evil was stupidity. The cure for it was knowledge based on scientific investigation."[21] Perhaps it never occurred to him that stupidity could not be cured by education, at least it did not in the beginning of his crusade.

In the spring of 1898 Du Bois completed his study, which the University of Pennsylvania published a year later. Titled *The Philadelphia Negro,* the study made Du Bois aware that "merely being born in a group, does not necessarily make one possessed of complete knowledge concerning it,"[22] a seminal fact that provides one rationale for Black Studies. At the end of the Philadelphia study, Du Bois announced his plan to study the "complete Negro problem in the United States."[23] He did not submit his study to the University of Pennsylvania until the spring of 1898, although he began teaching at Atlanta University in the fall of 1897. Apparently, Du Bois decided he would be able to introduce his idea at Atlanta University. He thought so for several reasons, mainly because he had been approached by Horace Bumstead, president of Atlanta University, requesting that Du Bois take charge of the work in sociology and the new conferences that were focused on the "Negro Problem."[24] Here was an opportunity that Du Bois had been searching for; and one that fit perfectly within his plans. The location in the South where the majority of the black population resided he also considered an advantage.

Du Bois, at last able to structure a program of sociology, promoted the idea of a "changing developing society rather than a fixed social structure."[25] At an address before the American Academy of Political and Social Science in 1897, Du Bois outlined the theoretical framework and practical means for studying black Americans.[26] He remained at Atlanta University, where he carried out this work for thirteen years, from 1897–1910. The significance of his work, according to Du Bois' own evaluation, was "a program of study on the problems affecting the American Negroes, covering a progressively widening and deepening effort designed to stretch over the span of a century."[27] He argued for the study of black Americans in order to advance the cause of science in general and to enlighten black people in particular.

The issues that arose between Du Bois and the avowed godfather of black higher education in the South, Booker T. Washington, did so gradually and over an extended period of time. In a letter dated July 27, 1894, Washington invited Du Bois to join the faculty at Tuskegee; and Du Bois might have accepted the offer had he not already committed himself to Wilberforce. While it is often said that the split between Washington and Du Bois took place following Washington's speech at the Atlanta Cotton States Exposition, such is not the case. On September 18, 1895, Du Bois wrote to Washington to say that Washington's speech made at the Cotton States Exposition was "a word fitly spoken."[28] At times Du Bois and Washington are described in oppositional terms, as in the famous Dudley Randall poem, "Booker T. and W.E.B."[29] However, following Washington's compromise speech, Du Bois not only wrote a congratulatory note, but in response to criticism of Washington in the black press, Du Bois wrote to *The New York Age* "suggesting that here might be the basis of a real settlement between whites and blacks in the South, if the South opened to the Negroes the doors of economic opportunity and the Negroes co-operated with the white South in political sympathy."[30]

Du Bois later claimed the offer or compromise was frustrated because between 1895 and 1909, blacks in the South were completely disfranchised. It would appear that Du Bois, a young man of twenty-seven, was perhaps naïve enough to believe the white South would abide by the compromise; or, as some have suggested,[31] he had his own agenda, because his thinking on the matter of political rights was clearly articulated in 1887 when as a Fisk student he wrote "An Open Letter to the Southern People," saying, "What we demand is to be recognized as men, and to be given those civil rights which pertain to our manhood."[32] When Du Bois considered leaving Wilberforce in 1896, he again wrote to Washington; and this time Washington responded quickly. However, the offer had come from the University of Pennsylvania for Du Bois to conduct a sociological study of the Seventh Ward in Philadelphia; so once again he declined Washington's offer.

The position at the University of Pennsylvania was for one year. When it ended, Du Bois found himself again looking for employment. This time his Harvard thesis advisor, Albert Bushnell Hart, asked Washington to make Du Bois another offer. Washington declined, and in 1897 Du Bois accepted the position of professor of history and economics at Atlanta University. However, in 1902 Washington again offered Du Bois a teaching position. Du Bois by then had his eye on the position of commissioner of education in the District of Columbia. He asked for a recommendation, which Washington provided but then asked Du Bois not to use. The problem was that Washington's cronies wanted their friend Robert Terrell, Mary Church Terrell's husband, appointed. Clearly, Booker Washington found himself in an awkward position. Having already stated that Du Bois was the most qualified for the position, the best that he could do was to ask him to not use the recommendation. Washington claimed using the letter would make it appear that Du Bois was applying for or seeking the commissioner position himself rather than being pursued for the appointment. In the end, neither Du Bois nor Terrell was hired.

Du Bois had begun to suspect Washington of chicanery back in 1899, when Du Bois organized the conference at Atlanta University on "The Negro in Business." Washington liked the idea and used it to start the National Negro Business League. He used the Tuskegee machine to undermine Du Bois' role as coordinator of local chapters and head of the Committee of Afro-American Council. Du Bois agreed to serve in this position if money for mailings would be provided. Washington maneuvered the funds away from Du Bois so that he would probably relinquish the position, which Du Bois did. Washington wanted Du Bois' extensive list of black businessmen, and Du Bois gave it to him.[33] However, he recognized Washington's shenanigans. The job offer from Washington was still on the table, but in April 1900 Du Bois turned down the position, stating that after visiting Tuskegee in February, he found it to be too rural. He also claimed it was never made clear exactly what he was to do at the Institute. Ambiguity regarding his position would probably weigh more heavily on his decision than the agrarian nature of Tuskegee, Alabama. Still, their relationship remained cordial; in fact, Washington's third wife, Margaret, was Du Bois' classmate at Fisk. Du Bois never intended to take the differences of opinion between himself and Washington into a public debate.

Du Bois, nevertheless, became involved in a growing debate with Booker T. Washington over not only the type of education that should be available to black youth, but, as Du Bois explained, "Contrary to most opinion, the controversy as it developed was not entirely against Mr. Washington's ideas, but became the insistence upon the right of other Negroes to have and express their ideas."[34] It was not merely disagreement with Washington's philosophy that brought about the vitriolic exchange. In 1940, looking back, Du Bois claimed the issue was so much larger than "a program of education"; it "was opposition to a system and that system was part of the economic development of the United States."[35] Perhaps it was in Du Bois' mind, but for the average person a large part of the argument centered on the education of blacks. Washington was not the only one to espouse vocational education for black youth, for—as historian Derrick Aldridge makes clear—Kelly Miller, a Howard University professor; Anna Julia Cooper of the acclaimed M Street/Dunbar High School in Washington, D.C.; Nannie Helen Burroughs, tagged the "female Booker T. Washington" of the National Training School for Women and Girls; and Alexander Crummell, Episcopal priest and one of the founders of the American Negro Academy were among the many educators, members of the "talented tenth," involved in the controversy. However, Du Bois and Washington were the most prominent.

While Du Bois perhaps perfected the art of protest in his writings that urged his readers to "agitate, protest, reveal the truth and refuse to be silenced,"[36] Booker Washington had long before perfected the art of accommodation. Washington had concluded that the way for black people to succeed in the United States, particularly in the South, was to lift themselves up by their own bootstraps and to concentrate their efforts on earning a living.[37] Compromise was part of his strategy long before the Atlanta speech. Du Bois could not and would not compromise on principle. Washington, who was twelve years Du Bois' senior, had been born into slavery. He grew up in the South and learned early to placate whites. In 1881, when he founded Tuskegee Institute, he assured the whites of Alabama that the education he would offer black Americans would not lure them from the farms, but would make them better farmers, would not spoil them for service in the white community, but would make them better servants.[38] At the Cotton States Exposition in Atlanta in 1895, Washington renounced social equality for black Americans and urged them to pursue careers in "agriculture, mechanics, in commerce, in domestic services, and in the professions."[39] Here again, Washington was not the only one to make these statements, just the most well known. Nannie Helen Burroughs (1879–1961) in her circa 1903 speech "12 Things the Negro Must Do for Himself," advocated what Steven Covey would popularize decades later, that is, to put "first things first." According to Burroughs as well as to the many other educators of the period, education was to come first. While she did not discount a liberal education, she was a strong supporter of industrial training and sought to professionalize domestic work for women.

Du Bois, on the other hand, had received the best in liberal arts education, knew the classics, taught Greek and Latin, and thought what Washington advocated was the "gospel of work and money."[40] Du Bois resented Washington's philosophy and said so. In 1898 he contradicted the statements made by the supporters of vocational education for Blacks that implied "college-bred Negroes" were unemployable. In a commencement address delivered at Fisk University, Du Bois told the young graduates that they should aspire to become doctors, lawyers, teachers, ministers, writers, artists, scientists;[41] that the well educated would be employed. Clearly Du Bois believed higher education was the way out of poverty, whereas Washington believed it was hard work and thrift. A subtle problem with Washington's plan was that people were being trained for jobs that were becoming obsolete. Arthur Sutherland makes the cogent argument that the country was changing so quickly that many of the occupations were of little value and would result in low-wage jobs. Examples were jobs as blacksmiths and laundresses.

In 1903 Du Bois openly criticized Washington's accommodationist posture by declaring:

> Mr. Washington distinctly asks that Black people give up, at least for the present, three things:—First, political power, second, insistence on civil rights, third, higher education of Negro youths,—and concentrate all their energies on industrial education, the accumulation of wealth, and the conciliation of the South. In these years since Booker T. Washington's Atlanta speech . . . there have occurred: The disfranchisement of the Negro, The legal creation of a distinct status of civil inferiority, [and] The steady withdrawal of aid from institutions for the higher training of the Negro.[42]

Although these events could not be directly blamed on Washington's speech, Du Bois charged that Washington's "propaganda" was extremely influential and certainly aided in their speedier accomplishment. He stressed that one cannot accommodate injustice. Many people thought the 1903 publication of *The Souls of Black Folk* was the point of no return in the Du Bois-Washington relationship. Bauerlein states that it was not and claims the final break came when Du Bois was forced to choose between Washington's opponents and the Wizard of Tuskegee.

According to Bauerlein, Du Bois taught summer school at Tuskegee in 1905; however, Lewis lists the date as July 6, 1903, when Du Bois lectured in the Institute's summer session. Washington traveled to a speaking event in Boston at an AME Zion church, where Monroe Trotter and others who opposed Washington staged a protest. Trotter was arrested and served jail time. Du Bois left Tuskegee at the end of his course, traveled to Boston, and stayed at Trotter's home. This was insulting to Washington, who suspected Du Bois was somehow behind the protest. In *Dusk of Dawn*, Du Bois asserts that he had no prior knowledge of Washington's meeting, nor did he have any idea there was a plan to heckle Washington. Du Bois states, "But when Trotter went to jail, my indignation overflowed. I did not always agree with Trotter then or later. But he was an honest, brilliant, unselfish man, and to treat as a crime that which was at worst mistaken judgment was an outrage."[43] Du Bois does not mention teaching at Tuskegee nor that he left Alabama and traveled to Boston. Whatever actually took place, the turmoil referred to in the press as the "Boston Riot" was the beginning of the end of Du Bois' effort to finesse his relationship with Washington. Washington forced his hand by turning a difference of opinion into a power struggle.[44]

After the break Du Bois organized the Niagara Movement, beginning in June 1905. The organization was incorporated in Washington, D.C., on January 31, 1906. Washington saw the Niagara Movement as a direct threat to the Tuskegee machine, and Du Bois was accused of being envious of Washington's status and power. Instead, Du Bois and the men of the movement demanded full political rights immediately. As regards to education they said, "We mean real education. We believe in work. We ourselves are workers, but work is not necessarily education. Education is the development of power and ideal."[45] The declaration goes on to say they would fight "for all time against any proposal to educate black boys and girls simply as servants and underlings, or simply for the use of other people."[46] Certainly, this flew in the face of Washington's gospel of work.

In the September 1896 issue of *The Atlantic*, Washington published "The Awakening of the Negro" in which he began with an example of a poor black boy reading a French grammar in front of an ill-kept cabin and another of parents who obviously sacrifice to rent a piano for their daughter's music lessons while they live in poverty. To Washington the behavior was ludicrous, while to Du Bois it represented freedom of choice. Parents often live in poverty and sacrifice pinning their hopes on the coming generation. For Du Bois the life of the mind was as important as the comforts of the body. Washington, however, believed that "a white man respects a Negro who owns a two-story house."[47] He understood the southern white people who feared free schools for "the freedmen and the poor whites—the education of the head alone—would result merely in increasing the class who sought to escape labor, and that the South would soon be overrun by the idle and vicious."[48] He assured them that Tuskegee would produce black people who are not afraid to work. Du Bois answered Washington in his 1902 essay, "Of the Training of Black Men." He asked,

> If after all the industrial school is the final and
> sufficient answer in the training of the Negro

race . . . [i]s not life more than meat, and the body more than raiment? And men ask this to-day all the more eagerly because of the sinister signs in recent educational movements. And above all, we daily hear that an education that encourages aspiration, that sets the loftiest of ideals and seeks as an end culture and character rather than bread-winning, is the privilege of white men and the danger and delusion of black.[49]

Du Bois wanted black youth to benefit from both industrial and liberal education.

In an interview with Ralph McGill of the *Atlanta Constitution*, perhaps the last interview he would grant, the ninety-four-year-old Du Bois asserted that he believed Washington's compromise speech in which he stated that blacks could be as separate as the fingers on his hand was responsible for the 1896 separate but equal ruling of *Plessey v Ferguson*. Du Bois accused Washington of advocating "industrial slavery" for Black people. He explained that is why he challenged other black men to rise up and oppose a course of action that would prevent or detour them from full citizenship even if their protest involved "disagreement with Mr. Booker T. Washington."[50] A major issue was that whites accepted Washington's views as those of all black people. He was the anointed spokesman.

Du Bois also told McGill that he believed Washington might have decided to accept the political status quo because he was disenchanted with the frustrations and failures of Frederick Douglass. Washington had watched the party of Lincoln cast off the freed blacks, watched the failure of Reconstruction, the historic compromise with southern whites that put Rutherford B. Hayes in the White

House in 1876; he effectively ended Reconstruction. Washington watched helplessly the federal troops abandon the newly freed. Du Bois said in the same interview, "Washington's decision may have lacked a certain idealism, but it was born out of a present reality."[51] Later in his life he also said, "I think that maybe the greatest difference between Booker T. and myself was that he had felt the lash, and I had not."[52] He understood how the differences in their lived experiences set them on different paths. All things considered, Du Bois thought Washington was sincere but wrong.

James D. Anderson's article "The Hampton Model of Normal School Industrial Education, 1868–1900" (1978) provides a background for viewing Du Bois' criticism of Washington. The article demonstrates that criticisms of Samuel Chapman Armstrong's program for training conservative black teachers to help adjust the black minority to a subordinate social and economic role in the South started in the middle 1870s and long pre-dated the debates between Du Bois and Washington.[53] Aldridge's research points out those white educators, namely Robert Ogden, J.L.M. Curry, and Thomas Jesse Jones who also supported black industrial education for the purpose of supplying the work force.[54] Furthermore, they lay the groundwork for the debates that would come at the turn of the century.

Du Bois believed each human being, regardless of color or creed, should receive the finest education available. He realized, of course, that everyone might not profit from a classical education, but he thought that those black people who could benefit most from a liberal education should receive it. Blacks with the best education would then use their knowledge to uplift the masses. This formed the basis of Du Bois' concept of the talented tenth. Du Bois claimed to have understood the need for what Washington did in order to gain financial support, but felt that he was giving up too much that would be too hard to win back. Washington "bartered away much that was not his to barter."[55] Du Bois believed that Washington in the last years of life recognized the damage he had done. He said that Washington kept hoping, but before he died he must have known that whites had betrayed him, and that without intending to he had helped them. Du Bois believed that Washington died "in sorrow and betrayal."[56]

Du Bois and Washington had more in common than might at first be apparent. As Lacy observed, both men fought against racist legislation, both fought for the removal of Jim Crow laws, both were in favor of black nationalism or racial self-help; although Washington's program was primarily economic and Du Bois' was political and cultural. Both men were committed to the black race. Du Bois, however, possessed a worldview, whereas Washington limited his concern to blacks in the American South. Washington depended on the goodwill of whites. Du Bois did not. And while he agreed with Washington that "blacks had to move cautiously in the South, he interpreted Washington's moves as submissive and degrading to black people."[57] In the true spirit of protest, his rhetoric reminiscent of Malcolm X and other members of the Nation of Islam, Du Bois declared: "I am resolved to be quiet and law-abiding, but to refuse to cringe in body or in soul, to resent deliberate insult, and to assert my just right in the face of wanton aggression."[58] Actually Malcolm X's stance echoed Du Bois.

When Booker T. Washington died in 1915, Du Bois was the foremost authority on black liberation, which makes his statement in the 1962 interview especially perplexing. Thinking about Washington's death Du Bois said,

"A lot of people think I died at the same time."[59] Without Washington's leadership, Tuskegee slowly faded into the background. Du Bois would now be able to unite all the groups fighting for black political rights under the NAACP banner. In 1916 he attempted to do exactly this at a conference held at Joel Spingarn's home in Amenia, New York, that brought together distinguished black leaders from across the country. For the first time in many years, the leaders expressed unanimity of opinion. Du Bois was elated that the number one resolution of the conference was presented as follows: The conference believes that all forms of education are desirable for the Negro and that every form of education should be encouraged and advanced.[60]

In his writing Du Bois had sought to give white people the correct information regarding black Americans in order to change white opinion of black people. Changing the opinion of whites, Du Bois thought, would result in the integration of blacks into the mainstream of American society. However, as his views changed, Du Bois was to be counted among the first black American leaders to adhere to the idea of "voluntary race segregation."[61] Much of his trouble with the NAACP resulted from his growing nationalism, and Pan-Africanism. In an early essay, "The Conservation of the Races," (1897), Du Bois sets forth the rationale for black nationalism and lays the groundwork for his developing views on Pan-Africanism. He stressed maintaining a separate culture and identity in order for black people to make a unique contribution to the world. Du Bois defined Pan-Africanism as "the intellectual understanding and cooperation among all groups of Negro descent in order to bring about the earliest possible time for the industrial and spiritual emancipation of the Negro peoples."[62]

It is unclear when Du Bois evolved into a Pan-Africanist. In the 1968 *Autobiography* he stated he did not know
when he became interested in Africa. At any rate, his interest in Africa was a rarity in his day. Unlike other Americans who look to their mother country because of their
experiences or those of their parents, Du Bois explained
there was no similar experience for blacks either through
their own experiences or that of their parents. This lack
of knowledge resulted in a lack of appreciation for Africa.
Because of the deliberate maligning of Africans as uncivilized, black people of Du Bois' generation were generally
uninterested if not hostile toward Africa.[63] While this
statement is true, there certainly are notable exceptions,
for there was Bishop Henry McNeil Turner, an advocate
of the Back to Africa Movement, and before him Martin
R. Delaney, not to mention the huge Garvey Movement
composed mainly of working class folk.

For millions, however, Africa was viewed with distaste
as a result of the distortions and absence of historical facts
regarding the so-called dark continent. Africans were
perceived of as savage subhuman beings, incapable of language, art, or culture.[64] They deserved to be colonized, as
they were incapable of governing themselves. The social
Darwinists of the time helped promulgate these beliefs by
asserting that if blacks did not survive, it was because they
were not "the fittest," and that the subjugation of black
people was the "natural order of things."[65] Du Bois refused
to accept the lies, half-truths, and distortions concerning Africa. He became interested in Africa, he claimed,
"by a sort of logical deduction."[66] Through his study and
research in history, he found the truth for himself, and the
truth resulted in his love for Africa and his growing belief
in Pan-Africanism. He saw the commonality in the black

struggle for freedom, whether in America or in Africa. He saw the relationship of black people to world affairs, particularly to colonialism.[67]

Du Bois is often credited for being the father of Pan-Africanism; however the idea for the first Pan-African Congress came from a West Indian lawyer, H. Sylvester Williams, not from Du Bois.[68] This black lawyer, who practiced in England, had associated with Africans and black Americans there. In 1900 he called distinguished blacks from the United States, Africa, and the West Indies to meet in London to discuss the problems of colonialism and racial discrimination. Therefore, *Pan-Africanism* was actually the brainchild of Williams. In 1908 Williams returned to Trinidad, where he died in March 1911, at the age of forty-two. It was Du Bois then who introduced the word *Pan-Africanism* into currency, who promoted the concept and nurtured it to maturity.[69] Du Bois was among the thirty-five black Americans who attended the conference in 1900 and was elected vice-president of the newly formed organization.[70] While others (J. Max Barber, and T. Thomas Fortune among them) made significant contributions to the idea of Pan-Africanism, Du Bois was the one to succeed in organizing a series of five conferences. These began in Paris in 1919 during the Peace Treaty negotiations following World War I and concluded unanimity of opinion in Manchester, England in 1945.[71]

The Pan-African Congress that Du Bois called in 1919 consisted of fifty-seven delegates and represented sixteen different black groups.[72] This congress presented the following resolutions: (1) the development of 200,000,000 Black people; (2) a Code of Laws for the international protection of Africans; (3) a permanent bureau to enforce the laws; (4) restoration of land and capital to Africans; (5) the abolition of slavery and forced labor; (6) education as a right of every African child; (7) a system of public health in each African state; (8) the right of Africans for home rule; (9) and an end to cultural and religious chauvinism in relationships between missionaries and Africans.[73] At this conference Du Bois also announced, "The world fight for black rights is on!"[74] In 1921 the congress met again in sessions held in London, Paris, and Brussels and forwarded another list of resolutions. Du Bois worked assiduously for resolution number three, which called for education in self-knowledge and for resolution number seven, which called for the establishment of an international institution for the study of black American problems.[75] Du Bois stated the ideas of the congress in no uncertain terms. In *The Crisis* magazine he proclaimed:

> The absolute equality of races,—physical, political and social—is the founding stone of world peace and human advancement. No one denies great differences among individuals of all races, but the voice of science, religion and practical politics is one in denying the God-appointed existence of super-races, or of races naturally and inevitably and eternally inferior.[76]

Unlike Marcus Garvey, Du Bois' idea of Pan-Africanisn was spiritual and philosophical. Du Bois advocated no mass return of black Americans to Africa, as did Garvey. On the idea of physically returning to Africa, Du Bois stated:

> Let us realize that we are Americans, that we were brought here with the earliest settlers, and that the very sort of civilization from which we

came made the complete adoption of western modes and customs imperative if we were to survive. There is nothing so indigenous, so completely "made in America" as we. It is as absurd to talk of a return to Africa, merely because that was our home 300 years ago, as it would be to expect the members of the Caucasian race to return to the vastness of the Caucasus Mountains from which, it is reputed, they sprang.[77]

Du Bois would change his mind as he did about many things. But in the beginning of his embrace of Africa he could not see returning to Africa as a viable choice. As a result of his position on Pan-Africanism, Du Bois once again became embroiled in debate. Marcus Garvey, a black man from Jamaica, West Indies, challenged Du Bois' leadership and laughed at his theoretical concept of Pan-Africanism.

Garvey has been described as possessing the best attributes of both Washington and Du Bois. He had Du Bois' radical spirit and Washington's rapport with the common man.[78] Consequently, he was extraordinarily popular. His organization, the Universal Negro Improvement Association (UNIA), headquartered in Harlem, boasted a membership that far exceeded the NAACP. Garvey's mission was, he believed, to "liberate Africa from all forms of European oppression and to make it free for all Africans and all people of African descent."[79] He advocated the return of all black people to their homeland—Africa, where he would become President! Historians[80] have noted that conflict between Du Bois and Garvey was unavoidable, for despite Du Bois' radicalism, he represented the NAACP, which did not seem especially relevant to the black masses. Lacy observes that the NAACP had achieved some impressive court victories, but the majority of blacks were not concerned with voting in white primaries, as important as that might have been. They had immediate material needs, and victories in high courts were too far removed to be of any practical benefit.[81]

Of course another reason Du Bois and Garvey were on a collision course had to do with the fact that what Garvey was advocating was a kind of black colonialism, setting himself up as president of Africa, speaking of Africa as though it were a single country instead of a diverse continent, and taking the hard-earned money of his followers for what to Du Bois seemed a bombastic plan doomed to fail. Garvey's plan did appeal to the masses because it addressed their concrete needs, offered them a way out of poverty, and showed them how to leave the land of racism where they experienced only second-class citizenship. In the beginning, Du Bois sought to ignore Garvey. But Garvey attacked Du Bois as a false leader of Black people and accused him of "worshipping the white man's symbols of progress."[82] While not entirely untrue, it probably was unnecessary for Garvey to say at the time.

Garvey and his followers branded the NAACP an elitist group of middle-class Blacks supported by liberal northern whites. According to Philip Foner (1970), Du Bois agreed with Garvey's major aims; but he reasoned and stated that Garvey was an idealist with an unworkable pipe dream. Du Bois also said Garvey's plan was "bombastic, wasteful, illogical and ineffective and almost illegal."[83] He criticized Garvey on the issue of social equality. Du Bois thought Garvey had no right to willingly accept the position that the United States belonged to white people, and that blacks should not fight for equality in American society. The debate between Garvey and Du Bois ended when Garvey was suddenly deported from the United States for mail fraud. Many of Garvey's followers blamed Du Bois and the NAACP for Garvey's deportation. As it turns out the FBI's J. Edgar Hoover was more to blame.

Du Bois in several articles in *The Crisis* stated his feelings about Garvey. "To sum up," he wrote, "Garvey is a sincere, hardworking, idealist; he is also a stubborn, domineering leader of the masses; he has worthy industrial and commercial schemes but he is an inexperienced businessman,[84] all of which was true. Du Bois characterized the Garvey Movement as "the most interesting spiritual movement of the modern Negro world."[85] Perhaps it is ironic that in the end Du Bois would emigrate to where Garvey wanted to take all black people and would develop a close relationship with Ghana's first president, Kwame Nkrumah, who was profoundly influenced by Marcus Garvey.[86]

During the 1920s Pan-Africanism meant for Du Bois what perhaps the first Zionist movement must have meant to Jews, "the centralization of race effort and the recognition of a racial fount."[87] But Du Bois' ideas on expatriation would change, at least as they pertained to him individually. He worked long and hard for the liberation of Africa from colonialism, because in African freedom he saw the amelioration of the conditions of black people throughout the world. Because the NAACP did not share Du Bois' philosophy of Pan-Africanism, the more pronounced his concern for Africa became the wider the gap between Du Bois and the organization grew. The situation was exacerbated by Du Bois' insistence that "the opposition to segregation is an opposition to discrimination. The experience in the United States has been that usually when there is racial segregation there is also racial discrimination."[88] This, he emphasized, need not always be the case. The fine points of distinction Du Bois stubbornly persisted in making between segregation and voluntary separation apparently were missed by the NAACP, and the issue eventually forced his resignation in 1934. Unlike his ideas about the talented tenth, Pan-Africanism was a philosophy Du Bois never abandoned. As he grew older he expanded, refined, and intensified his ideas to fuse with the other philosophies he was to embrace.

As early as 1904, Du Bois was interested in the ideas of socialism. But it was not until 1957 that he would write that the one hope of American Negroes was socialism.[89] Through the years Du Bois had moved from his advocacy of individualism, the work ethic, thrift, and savings to the realization that group economy and not private business enterprise was necessary for the protection and welfare of black Americans. Between his first interest in Socialist concepts and his full endorsement of that ideology, he toyed with ideas of consumer advocacy and cooperation. The consumer groups in which Du Bois was involved failed. They failed, he believed, because they lacked the support of the state.[90] In an article entitled "Negroes and Socialism," Du Bois asserted that half the world, including the United States, embraced some form of socialism.[91] He pointed out that half the world owned all capital and had abolished private profit. Black Americans who stood to gain the most from a Socialist form of government were, according to Du Bois, ignorant of this ideology and kept so deliberately. In still another article he argued for the establishment of a welfare state that would benefit black Americans and other poor people. He advocated more public ownership and said that public power should not be maintained by private corporations.[92]

In college and during his political inclination toward what was known as black protest, Du Bois saw socialism as an "amelioration of the wages contract, more humane relations between employer and employee, but it involved no fundamental study of Marxists."[93] Beyond this," he said, he "was not thinking."[94] Later, in graduate school in Berlin, Du Bois explored socialism and attended meetings of the Socialist party. In a letter dated October 1, 1961, he wrote that as a student in Berlin he considered himself a Socialist.[95] However, this statement is not substantiated in any of his other writings, including the autobiographies. Furthermore, in 1907 Du Bois stated he was a Socialist-of-the-path, meaning that he did not embrace the complete abolition of private property in capital—but the path of progress and common sense should certainly lead to a far greater ownership of public wealth for the public good than was presently the case.[96]

As early as 1904, Du Bois summarized the black problem in the United States as a series of unjust and dangerous economic conditions. He sympathized with the Socialist movement, yet he was keenly aware of the problems facing socialism in a biracial society. Racial caste and economic class were recognizably in conflict. American capitalists were eager, Du Bois charged, to reap the profits to be made by exploiting racial hatred. The Socialist stand was that there was nothing special about the "Negro question." Du Bois disagreed. Regardless of the shortcomings in the Socialist program, in 1911 he joined the Socialist party,[97] although he resigned in 1912 and supported Woodrow Wilson for president. Du Bois refused to accept the Socialist explanation that the "Negro question" was simply a problem of the working class. A letter from Isaac Max Rubinow, a Socialist economist, stated the Socialist position clearly, declaring "that only through emancipation of the whole working class can the emancipation of the Negro be brought about."[98] Du Bois thought the Marxist theory needed modification in the United States, for he perceived that blacks were exploited by whites, both the capitalist and the proletariat.

During much of his Socialist period, Du Bois hoped that capitalism could and would reform itself. But in 1961, he described capitalism as "universal selfishness" and was convinced that it was a system that would one day self-destruct. He concluded, finally, that the system could not reform itself. The Socialists in America had not been able to eradicate racism from organized labor unions. Therefore, Du Bois never fully embraced the Socialist party. He observed that from 1872 to 1924 the plight of the American black laborer was never specifically mentioned in the party platform.[99] Despite the contradictions in the party, Du Bois still accepted the principles of socialism. He saw that the world was changing and comprehended that the global economic organization was of primary importance.[100]

Some of Du Bois' loss of faith in capitalism developed after World War I. Disillusioned by the Depression of 1893 and World War I in 1926 he began visiting Communist lands. He, unlike many other Americans, had both the opportunity and the desire to see for himself how other governments functioned. He went to the Soviet Union in 1926, 1936, 1949, and again in 1959.[101] He also visited East Germany, Czechoslovakia, and Poland; spent ten weeks in China and a month in Rumania. His travels clearly influenced his political opinions.

In 1953 Du Bois lectured "On the Future of the American Negro." This visionary address warned black Americans of the extreme shortsightedness of the capitalistic approach to life. Du Bois explained that:

> Whereas in the nineteenth century the world thought that progress and emancipation were coming from popular education and universal suffrage, we now know that more fundamental than these important rights is the economic organization of the world; the way in which the labor of human beings is organized to satisfy human needs. This question is so fundamental that all other questions of political power, education and human happiness depend upon it. This is the basic reason for the rise of philanthropy, socialism, and the attempt at complete realization of socialism through communism. Most American Negroes of education and property have long since oversimplified their problem and tried to separate it from all other social problems. They conceive that their fight is simply to have the same rights and privileges as other American citizens. They do not for a moment conceive that the economic organization of America may have fundamental injustices and shortcomings which seriously affect not only Negroes, but the world. Just as Booker T. Washington in his day assumed that American ideals were complete and right, and that all we had to do was to fight to imitate and attain them, so today we Negroes are largely quite swept away by the miracles of American industry, the huge accumulation of wealth, and the conspicuous expenditure which we find about us.[102]

Du Bois saw black Americans as an important segment of the American working class, but more than that, he saw them as a force that should join in and support the world population that was fighting for better economic organizations. The paradox of capitalism, as Du Bois saw it, was that capitalist ambition led to the aspiration for higher income brackets, and progress was seen as escaping from manual labor to white-collar jobs and then to employing others to work for the capitalist while he or she arranged to have nothing to do. Du Bois concluded that "poverty in the worker must be perpetuated in order that he be compelled to work for the rich."[103] While Du Bois never again joined the Socialist party, he advanced the notions of socialism and worked to incorporate Socialist ideals into the struggle for black equality.

Du Bois' own ideas seem in some ways contradictory. For example, his statement about the avoidance of work and the aspiration toward "white-collar" or professional jobs certainly echoes Washington's 1896 statement about the dignity of hard work in "The Awakening of the Negro." Washington argued that higher education could lead to idle and vicious attempts to escape labor. Both seem to argue that there is dignity in manual labor, and of course there is; but in all of its dignity few want to engage, including both Washington and Du Bois.

On the first day of October 1961, Du Bois applied for membership in the Communist party of the United States. He was, as he stated himself, "long and slow in coming to this decision."[104] The events that led to this decision were many and often complicated by the fact of Du Bois's race. One can but wonder how he would analyze the collapse of the Soviet Union or, for that matter, the economic downturn in capitalist countries including the United States were he alive today.

During the 1950s the United States underwent an hysterical reaction to the very idea of communism. Anyone thought to be Communist or Socialist came under attack. The Internal Security Act of 1950 restricted the right of Communists to hold federal jobs and to work in defense plants. In 1954 the Communist Control Act outlawed the Communist party, and in the late 1950s Communists were convicted for not registering under the Internal Security Act.[105] In 1957 the House Committee on Un-American Activities listed 733 organizations and publications considered communistic or Communist fronts. Du Bois, who was vice-chairman of the Council on African Affairs, came under attack from the United States government.[106]

The Council on African Affairs had been organized in 1939 by Max Yergan, a black American secretary of the YMCA, and by Paul Robeson, the acclaimed singer and actor. The council was a New York-based group that raised funds for striking South African miners, gave lectures on African history and culture, and functioned basically as a Pan-African organization. It was neither Communist nor Socialist, but a few of its members were.[107] The United States government identified the Council on African Affairs as a subversive group.

Du Bois continued to work with the organization despite its label. Always an outspoken critic of the United States, he had often attacked its form of government, identifying capitalism as an extreme form of selfishness. Lacy (1970) points out several of Du Bois' critical statements, for example, "American democracy fails to function."[108] He said the cure for the social problems he had outlined was "to change the socially planned United States into a welfare state."[109] He exhorted American people "to take over the control of the nation in industry as well as government."[110] And if this were not enough, he insisted, "If this be treason, make the most of it."[111] The government would do just that. In addition to his statements, which were viewed by the government as inflammatory, Du Bois published exclusively (no one else would accept his manuscripts) in far left journals such as *New Africa, Masses and Mainstream,* and *The National Guardian.*[112]

Finally, another issue that cast a shadow of suspicion on Du Bois during the McCarthy era was the fact that he had in 1950 become chairman of the Peace Information Center.[113] The PIC was considered a "flagrantly subversive group."[114] The government charged that the PIC was "acting as an agent for a foreign principal without having filed its registration statement."[115] Du Bois denied the allegations and accused the Department of Justice of being unwise enough to "deal cavalierly with the rights of American citizens."[116] Du Bois ran for the United States Senate on the Progressive party ticket in 1950 and, surprising even himself, won 205,000 of the 5 million votes.[117]

In 1950 the Department of Justice demanded that Du Bois register as an agent of a foreign government.[118] He refused. The PIC sent a statement that set forth Du Bois' position. The statement read:

> The Peace Information Center is American in its conception and formation. Its activities were intended to and do relate only to the people of the United States. It acts and is responsible only to itself and to the people of this country. It has never agreed, either by contract or otherwise, to act as a "publicity agent" for a "foreign principal" as defined in the Act, nor does it purport or assume to act as one.[119]

On October 12, 1950, members of the Board of Advisors voted to dissolve the PIC. Du Bois stated that they had "no intention of running counter to the government, but only wished to make it clear that we did not believe we should register under the law."[120] In spite of this disbandment, Du Bois was indicted on February 9, 1951, for not registering as an agent of a foreign power in the peace movement. He was tried on November 8, 1951, in Washington, D.C. However, the case was never allowed to go to a jury. The judge acquitted all persons indicted, stating that the prosecution had failed to prove or offer any support or evidence to substantiate the charge in the indictment.[121] After a nine-month ordeal, Du Bois was finally free. Unfortunately, he felt he had been found guilty long before he had his day in court. He had lost many friends who were afraid of government action, he had been found guilty in the press, and even after his acquittal, he continued to be suspect.[122] In *Black Leadership* (1998) Marable details the activities of Walter White and the NAACP's refusal to support Du Bois, one of their founding members.

Du Bois' trials seemed to intensify his fighting spirit. With the publication of his ironically titled book *In Battle for Peace* (1952), he openly thanks the Communists of the world for their help in his defense, and his clear stand in favor of the Soviet Union in turn intensified the enmity of those who opposed him. In his speeches and in his writings he defended Julius and Ethel Rosenberg, who were eventually executed on charges they conspired to commit espionage; and he continued to oppose the mistreatment of people who forwarded unpopular or opposing views regarding the United States government.[123]

Du Bois charged that the federal government, in retaliation for his continued defiance, kept him under surveillance, declared his neighborhood "out of bounds" for Soviet diplomats, caused reputable commercial publishers to continue to refuse his manuscripts, had his mail tampered with or withheld, and warned black American newspapers not to carry his writings or to mention his name.[124] A whispering campaign continually intimated that some hidden treason or bribery could be placed at Du Bois' door had the government not been lenient.[125] The NAACP that he had helped to found, and for which he had worked for twenty-eight years, refused to allow local branches to invite him to events or permit him to lecture at their events. He was even refused the right to speak on a University of California campus because of NAACP protest.[126] To summarize his unjust treatment, Du Bois wrote: "In time I was rejected of men, refused the right to travel abroad and classed as [sic] 'controversial figure' even after being acquitted of guilt by a Federal court of law."[127]

His beliefs, his outspoken honesty, his defiance, all caused Du Bois to suffer greatly, but his experiences did not break his indefatigable spirit. At eighty-four years old, he continued to speak and write, found new friends, faced his lowered income and lived within it. He had lost the leadership of his race, and by this Du Bois was especially saddened; but he conceded:

> It was a dilemma for the mass of Negroes; either they joined current beliefs and actions of most whites or they could not make a living or hope for preferment. Preferment was possible. The color line was beginning to break. Negroes were getting recognition as never before. Was not the sacrifice of one man, small payment for this? Even those who disagreed with this judg-

ment at least kept quiet. The colored children ceased to hear my name.[128]

His stepson, David Graham Du Bois, stated that Du Bois, never one to "pontificate" but definitely opinionated, fell silent during the trauma of his ordeal.[129] In a period of deep contemplation he came to decisions that would govern the rest of his life.

In 1953, Du Bois was awarded a $7,000.00 peace prize by the World Peace Council.[130] Later he was awarded the Lenin Peace Prize, but could not travel to receive it because the United States government would not release his passport.[131] In retrospect, Du Bois was stunned by the fact that working for peace would lead to so much turmoil. Long before the turn of the century, he had warned that Americans were lacking "a certain hard commonsense in facing the complicated phenomena of political life."[132] He pointed out:

> We have the somewhat inchoate idea that we are not destined to be harassed with great social questions, and that even if we are, and fail to answer them, the fault is with the question and not with us. Consequently, we often congratulate ourselves more on getting rid of a problem than on solving it. Such an attitude is dangerous; we have and shall have, as other peoples have had, critical, momentous, and pressing questions to answer. The riddle of the Sphinx may be postponed, it may be evasively answered now; sometime it must be fully answered.[133]

Although Du Bois wrote the above statement in the late nineteenth century, it was especially relevant to the 1950s, and even to today.

In July 1958 the Supreme Court handed down a decision that said: "Congress had never given the Department of State any authority to demand a political affidavit as prerequisite to issuing a passport."[134] As a result of this decision, the State Department was forced to issue passports to several persons, including Du Bois, who previously had been denied the right to travel. Du Bois was now ninety years old, and when he received his passport, he said he felt like a "released prisoner."[135] He planned immediately to travel abroad. He and his second wife, Shirley Graham, went first to England, then to Holland, France, the Soviet Union, China; and they spent May Day in Moscow. They also attended the tenth session of the World Council of Peace in Stockholm. On July 1, 1959, they returned to the United States.[136] Du Bois wrote that this trip had a profound influence on his thinking.

In Western Europe Du Bois discovered that a people who had suffered from war and its destruction wanted to hear nothing of peace. Furthermore, he found no European labor party ready to help emancipate the workers of Asia or Africa. He observed that:

> On the contrary, all are willing to take higher wages based on colonial profits; and to fight wars waged to defend those profits. Back of this attitude of Western Europe is the United States: ready with funds to help Europe; ready to assist any European power to keep control of colonial peoples, or to supplant it as colonial ruler.[137]

In the Soviet Union Du Bois interviewed Prime Minister Khrushchev, and they discussed the Pan-African Movement.[138] Since Du Bois was still advocating Black Studies, in Moscow he suggested establishing an Academy of Sciences to study African history and culture. This was to be an institute for the study of Pan-African history, sociology, ethnography, anthropology, and all cognate studies. In Russia Du Bois' dream for the institute was realized. The institute was subsequently established with his friend Ivan Potekhin as director.[139] The Institute for African Studies is part of the Russian Academy of Science in Moscow. Potekhin died in 1964, but the institute survived and marked its fiftieth anniversary in October 2009.[140] Of his 1959 trip Du Bois noted:

> The Soviet Union is great and growing greater, and as it seems to believe, it belongs to this two hundred million folk about me. I am strongly inclined to agree with them. . . . Our increasing number of visitors to Russia see a contented people who do not hate the United States, but fear its war-making, and are eager to cooperate with us. From such a nation we can learn.[141]

Whether or not one agrees with Du Bois' idea about the economic organization of the world, his sincerity towards achieving world peace can hardly be doubted; nor can the fact be dismissed that he saw himself as a citizen of the world. Du Bois also praised China, where he witnessed the work of women who were achieving greater freedom.[142]

W.E. Burghardt Du Bois capped his political life in the United States by joining the Communist party. At the age of ninety-three, Du Bois, having studied socialism and communism in countries where they were practiced, having read widely and conducted the research of a scholar for over half a century, came finally to the following conclusion:

> I believe in communism. I mean by communism, a planned way of life in the production of wealth and work designed for building a state whose objective is the highest welfare of its people and not merely the profit of a pact. I believe all men should be employed according to their ability and that wealth and services should be distributed according to need. Once I thought those ends could be attained under capitalism, means of production in accord with free individual initiative. After earnest observation I now believe that private ownership of capital and free enterprise are leading to world disaster.... I resent the charge that communism is a conspiracy: Communists often conspire as do capitalists. But it is false that all communists are criminal and that communism speaks and exists mainly by means of force and fraud. I shall therefore hereafter help the triumph of communism in every honest way that I can: without deceit or hurt; without war; and with goodwill to all men of all color, classes and creeds . . . the triumph of communism will be a slow and difficult task, involving mistakes of every sort. It will call for progressive change in human nature and a better type of manhood than is common today. I believe this is possible.[143]

Having finally joined the party, Du Bois left the United States in 1961 for Ghana, the first West African nation to gain its independence (1957). Du Bois never again returned to live in the United States of America.

While it may seem somewhat of a paradox, Du Bois never intended to engage in politics. In his final autobiography (published posthumously in 1968) he said that having been "reared in the New England tradition of regarding politics as no fit career for a man of serious aims and particularly unsuitable for a college-bred man,"[144] he had sought to avoid politics except for participation as a "voter, thinker, writer, and, on rare occasions as speaker."[145] Yet, before his life ended he had run for political office, become a political prisoner, and suffered greatly as a result of his political beliefs. Many of Du Bois' critics suggested that the impact of his personality and works on America and the world has been detrimental to the best interest of his native land.[146] Others, such as Francis Broderick (1958), seemed to pity him. Broderick wrote, "W.E.B. Du Bois is a lonely and tragic Negro. Once a national audience, black and white, heard his plea for Negro equality. Now few listen and fewer still heed him."[147] Still, there were those who understood Du Bois' effort to awaken the American conscience. Truman Nelson was one such friend. He declared:

> From the towering and broad-margined plateau of his prophecy, Du Bois could see Africa, the Negro homeland, where the black man really was the majority . . . Du Bois has been rewarded as this country nearly always rewards its prophets. He was arrested—as Thoreau was arrested, and Theodore Parker and Garrison. . . . Some day the people of this country will demand that their own records be set straight, and alongside the political accidents, the Presidents and Senators, will go the enduring and usable truths of

the American Prophets. Among these Prophets
will be W.E.B. Du Bois.[148]

In the final years of his life it is quite possible that he
welcomed exile. Those close to him seemed to think the
invitation of Ghana's new president, Dr. Kwame Nkrumah,
asking Du Bois to become director of the Encyclopedia
Africana project invigorated him.[149] He accepted the invitation and the position and lived the rest of his life happily
in self-imposed exile.[150]

In 1909 Du Bois, while still teaching at Atlanta University, had attempted to launch an Encyclopedia Africana
but could not secure the necessary funds for the project.
After Ghana, formerly known as the Gold Coast under
British colonial rule, gained its independence, its president
provided funds for the project in 1961 and appointed Du
Bois director. Du Bois grew to love the country where he
lived and worked and was neither attacked for his beliefs
nor avoided because of his skin color. On February 15,
1963, W.E.B. Du Bois renounced his American citizenship
and became a citizen of Ghana. On the day he received
the Certificate of Naturalization, he wrote the following
message to the minister of interior of Ghana:

> My great-grandfather was carried away in
> chains from the Gulf of Guinea. I have returned
> that my dust shall mingle with the dust of my
> forefathers. There is not much time left for me.
> But now, my life will flow on in the vigorous
> young stream of Ghanaian life which lifts the
> African personality to its proper place among
> men. And I shall not have lived and worked in
> vain.[151]

His life was long and varied, his education liberal, and he had traveled the world; thus, almost a century of experiences brought Du Bois to his final life choices. On his ninety-fifth birthday Du Bois was the recipient of the University of Ghana's first honorary degree. He celebrated with Ghana's first family.[152]

On August 27, 1963, as many black people in the United States gathered under the shadow of the Lincoln Memorial for the historic March on Washington, Du Bois died in Accra, Ghana. He died almost 100 years after the Emancipation Proclamation was signed. He had witnessed the death of Jim Crow laws, the beginning of school integration, two world wars, the Great Depression, and finally the independence of a colonized African nation.

CHAPTER 3

THE SOUL OF DU BOIS

I will be black as blackness can/ the blacker the mantle the mightier the man./ I am the smoke king, I am black.

—from *Song of the Smoke,* 1899

In 1881 Frederick Douglass wrote "The Color Line," in which he stated that undesirable conditions were deliberately linked to color. "When these [conditions] shall cease to be coupled with color, there will be no color line drawn."[1] In 1903 Du Bois responded saying that the problem of the twentieth century would be the color line. The color line that circumscribed the lives of black people was a plague on Du Bois' soul. He devoted his entire adult life to solving the problem of color in the United States and around the world. He tried every available means, including education, economics, ethics/social justice, democracy, socialism, and finally even communism to solve the problems of color prejudice and racism. What he left is a staggering collection of studies and writings that can be used as road maps in charting that special field of study known as Black Studies.

W.E.B. Du Bois' contributions to the development of Black Studies is to be found in his scientific investigation of the black experience in the United States and later in the Diaspora and in Africa, and in his thought-provoking essays that constitute a theoretical base for examining issues confronting Black Studies. Du Bois believed that, by compiling factual information concerning his fellow blacks, he could help other Americans to recognize the humanity, intelligence, and potential of the people they had enslaved for over two hundred years. He believed, perhaps naively and idealistically, that knowledge would eradicate injustice, prejudice, and racism. He sought to correct stereotypes with facts, to replace opinion with scientific evidence. Thus, as his career began, Du Bois embarked upon a plan that today serves as a blueprint for the multidisciplinary field of Black Studies. In 1896 he approached the United States commissioner of labor with a proposal to study blacks in a small Virginia town.[2] The proposal was reviewed by Carroll D. Wright, then commissioner, who agreed to publish it, providing he liked it.[3]

The Department of Labor Reports (1898, 1901) and *The Philadelphia Negro* (1899) mark the beginning of Du Bois' investigations. The Virginia study, "The Negroes of Farmville," appeared in the United States Bureau of Labor Bulletin in 1898.[4] The study was conducted during July and August of 1897 and became the first in a series of investigations of small, well-defined groups of black people in various parts of the United States.[5] The territory studied was fifty-seven miles southwest of Richmond, a predominantly black area consisting of sharecroppers. Du

Bois investigated the economic conditions of the blacks in Farmville. In concluding this study, he pointed out that the number of single women was larger than expected, the percentage of single black men over fifteen years of age was larger than the number of single men over fifteen years of age in Great Britain, France, Germany, Hungary, or Italy. This point was significant because the current assumption was that the black American population was dying out and would not survive beyond the turn of the century.[6] The facts and figures in this study brought to light things that were positive, negative, and indifferent. Du Bois ended his study by writing:

> One thing is clear, and that is the growing differentiation of classes among Negroes, even in small communities. This most natural and encouraging result of 30 years' development has not yet been sufficiently impressed upon general students of the subject, and leads to endless contradiction and confusion. For instance, a visitor might tell us that Negroes of Farmville are idle, unreliable, careless with their earnings, and lewd; another visitor might say that Farmville Negroes are industrious, owners of property, and slowly but steadily advancing in education and morals. These apparently contradictory statements made continually of Negro groups all over the land are both true to a degree, and become mischievous and misleading only when stated without reservation and assumed to be true of a whole community. The question then becomes, not whether the Negro is lazy and criminal or industrious and ambitious, but rather what in a given community is the proportion of lazy to industrious Negroes,

of paupers to property holders, and what is the tendency of development in these classes.[7]

On the basis of the information gathered in the Farmville study, Du Bois asserted that the industrious and property-accumulating class of blacks represented, on the whole, the tendencies of that group. However, he added, "The mass of sloth and immorality is still large and threatening."[8] Finally, he pointed out that the only way to ascertain how far the Farmville study could be generalized was with additional research. Du Bois' studies differed from the conferences held at Hampton and Tuskegee Institutes which were, according to Jonathan Grossman, "inspirational conferences" and "propaganda for social uplift."[9] In contrast, Du Bois intended to be objective and to reveal truth whether his findings proved positive or negative.

Du Bois' second study for the Department of Labor appeared as "The Negro in the Black Belt: Some Social Sketches."[10] This investigation consisted of six small groups totaling 920 black people who lived in Georgia. Unlike the first research, "Black Belt" was conducted by students in the senior class at Atlanta University. This too was a study of economic conditions. Du Bois thought the student investigators' added perception enhanced the work because they had experienced first hand the conditions that they investigated, and he said so in the introduction. The findings revealed that larger families tended to live in the country and smaller families in town, most of the children in both areas could read and write a little, and youth were migrating in large numbers to the cities of Atlanta and Macon. "The mass of Negroes," Du Bois wrote, "are hard-working people with small wages. Many, however, manage to buy homes with their savings. Yearly income is between $100 and $300 a year."[11] These Georgia families represented for Du Bois the hope of American blacks, and a solution to the so-called black problem. They were law-abiding, property-holding people who worked hard and sought to educate their children, thus disproving many of the stereotypes held about them.[12]

Du Bois was not the only person to submit studies on Black Americans to the Department of Labor, for during the period near the end of the nineteenth century other reports offer interesting comparisons. For example, William Taylor Thom, Ph.D., conducted research on "The Negroes of Sandy Springs, Maryland: A Social Study."[13] While the form of his research followed that used by Du Bois, the conclusions differ. Thom, a white researcher, centered his research on the free blacks in an agricultural community near Washington, D.C. He reported that this population was more religious and less hopeful about the future than the blacks in Farmville. In another study Thom concluded that the black people in Litwalton, Virginia, a community of oyster workers, were not as successful as they should have been because economic opportunity came too easily for them.[14]

The other researchers who reported to the Department of Labor were mainly white, and Du Bois believed they brought to the studies their biases based upon their educational experience, the Darwinian philosophy pervading the day, and their political and historical life experiences. Because of these barriers to an unbiased evaluation of the black experience by white researchers, brought particularly by southern white researchers, Du Bois reasoned that the task must be taken up by Black students, scholars, and researchers who would perhaps bring a much-needed sensitivity to the scientific studies. J. Branford Laws' report in 1902, "The Negro of Cinclare Central Factory and

Calumet Plantation, Louisiana,"[15] provided an example of the kind of research Du Bois resented. The conclusion of this report is worth quoting:

> The light-hearted hopefulness or the absence of care which so agreeably characterized the race a couple of generations ago seems to be disappearing. The younger generations are not on as good terms with the whites as their elders, and they know it and show it. In trouble they are helpless. They lack confidence in themselves and are not ingenious in finding expedients. Very few of them appear capable of deep emotion; sorrow over the dead dies with the sun; resentment passes with the night; of gratitude and local attachment they know nothing. Yet they are faithful servants. They are grossly animal in their sexual relations.[16]

Clearly racist and unscientific, this "study" was an example of the bias in social science with regard to black people.

In his third study, "The Negro Landholder of Georgia," Du Bois demonstrated that black Americans in Georgia had steadily acquired property since the war. Georgia had the largest black population of any state in the union, and it also included a greater diversity of social and physical conditions.[17] Georgia, this study revealed, was the only state that had kept a detailed record of black landholdings extending over a quarter of a century. According to Du Bois, this third study was an attempt to make clear the steps by which 470,000 black American freedmen and their children had, in one of the former slave states, gained possession of over a million acres of land in a generation (Du Bois 1901).

In 1906 Du Bois asked the commissioner of labor to authorize a study of another black community. This time he selected Lowndes County, Alabama. The study was approved by the department, and Du Bois conducted it with the assistance of Monroe Work, R.R. Wright, and about a dozen local employees. When the work was completed the department paid him $2,000, but the study was never published.[18] Du Bois was informed the study would not be published because "it touched on political matters,"[19] a reason often offered for not establishing Black Studies in higher education. When Du Bois asked for the report he found it had actually been destroyed. Prior to this occurrence, Du Bois proposed a massive plan for the study of black people and had received an encouraging reply from Carroll O. Wright, head of the Federal Bureau of Labor Statistics.[20] Du Bois had planned multiple studies, including the industrial development of black Americans, domestic service in a particular city, blacks in the professions in several cities, farm laborers in a typical agricultural region, the black church as a social institution in certain cities, and graduates of southern schools. In addition, he intended to study the attitude of organized labor toward black stevedores and other black workers, and develop a bibliography concerning the economic condition of blacks since emancipation.[21] Before these plans could be realized, however, Wright left the bureau, and his successor saw no value in the work. Thus, Du Bois decided to concentrate his efforts in the academic arena, bringing Black Studies into higher education.

In 1898, speaking before the American Academy of Political and Social Science, Du Bois said the university was the proper agent for Black Studies and that the University of Pennsylvania had already taken the lead in this regard by initiating a study on the blacks in Philadelphia. Du Bois had, in fact, completed the study of the Philadelphia Negro while he was soliciting the Labor Department to do more studies of this nature in other locations.

Aptheker (1977) described the Philadelphia study as an empirical, detailed study of urban life, with concerns about class stratification and an insistence upon the consequence of social environment upon human behavior. *The Philadelphia Negro* is a seminal work in Black Studies and sociology. Lester (1971) called the study "the first systematic attempt to scientifically analyze and understand a black community."[22] The Philadelphia study presented every aspect of black American life, history, demography, family, migration, education, occupations, health, organized life, crime, prison, pauperism, alcoholism, housing, amusements, class differentiation, contact with whites, voting, and other political activity. Interestingly, Du Bois combined his ability as an historian with his perceptiveness as a social scientist and included a historical perspective that examined past conditions in order to provide an understanding of the present conditions. While conducting this study, Du Bois and his young bride from Cedar Rapids, Iowa lived in the 7th ward, the ghetto under investigation.

The Philadelphia Negro included a map of the 7th ward, a five-page bibliography, and an appendix that contained the questions used in the house-to-house survey. Du Bois concluded that the so-called race problem in Philadelphia was actually a problem of the poor and dispossessed. He pointed out that racism costs the city something. He believed that prejudice was a vast factor in aiding and abetting crime. In his recommendations he asked black people to work to solve their own problems by contributing to their poor, paying their share of the taxes, and by supporting the schools and public administration. To accomplish this he said they had a right to demand freedom for self-development and self-determination.[23] To the whites he said:

> The white people of the city must remember that much of the sorrow and bitterness that surrounds the life of the American Negro comes from the unconscious prejudice and half-conscious actions of men and women who do not intend to wound or annoy. Without doubt social differences are facts not fancies and cannot lightly be swept aside; but they hardly need to be looked upon as excuses for downright meanness and incivility.[24]

To both races, Du Bois asserted that black people were in the United States to stay; this being the case, it was in the best interest of both races for black people to achieve their highest potentials, for to not do so was detrimental to the whole society. black people should make every effort at self-improvement. Every white person should guard "their civilization against debauchment by themselves or others."[25] However, in order to do this, according to Du Bois, it was not necessary for whites to retard the efforts of earnest people to rise. The young Du Bois clearly was enamored of white culture and appeared to believe that white culture was something for black people to emulate. "With these duties in mind and with a spirit of self-help, mutual aid and co-operation, the two races should strive side by side to realize the ideals of the republic and make this truly a land of equal opportunity for all men."[26] While he does not say so outright, assimilation appears to be the intended outcome of such co-operation.

The conclusion of the study made it clear that the facts gathered concerning the black people in Philadelphia could not and should not be generalized to Blacks in Atlanta or elsewhere. Therefore, Du Bois repeatedly stressed the need for further study. The Atlanta University Studies was his plan to study the facts, any and all facts, concerning the plight of black people in the United States, and by measurement and comparison and research, reach any valid generalizations.[27] His main objective was to conduct this work with scientific accuracy, for he believed without it his results would be invalid. Because he also firmly believed Black Americans were a dynamic racial group, he embraced the concept of a changing developing society, rather than a fixed social structure.[28]

In 1896, Du Bois was thrilled when approached by President Horace Bumstead of Atlanta University and asked to come to Atlanta to conduct work in sociology and to direct the new conferences which the university was inaugurating on Black problems. Eventually Atlanta University initiated research on the urban Blacks, preceded a few years earlier in 1894 by Hampton and Tuskegee Institutes which had begun studies on the rural Blacks.[29]

When Du Bois took charge of the Atlanta Conferences in 1897, one conference had been held and another planned. These followed the Hampton and Tuskegee conference models which were primarily directed toward specific social reform efforts. Under Du Bois' leadership the concept of the conferences changed substantially. His effort was more academic in nature. He focused on the scientific investigation of social conditions, primarily for scientific ends. He put no special emphasis on reform effort, but wanted to expand and increase the collection of a basic body of facts concerning the social condition of Blacks.

The Atlanta University Studies consisted of annual conferences which focused on a series of research reports concerning various aspects of the Black experience in the South. The results of the conferences were put into pamphlet form and distributed at a nominal price. Du Bois became editor of these publications in 1898 with the third publication. The first Atlanta University Publication appeared in 1896, and was entitled "Mortality Among Negroes in Cities." The publication included reports of investigations conducted by various Black men and women, graduates of Atlanta University, and professionals in the city of Atlanta that included physicians, nurses, teachers, and social workers. Dr. H. R. Butler documents why Black Americans were dying at a rate faster than whites, by pointing to the small wooden Grady Hospital Annex by the kitchen with 50 or 60 beds for 40,000 Black citizens who were expected to receive medical care there. Butler also blames the superstitions and ignorance of black people, the high risk and unsanitary jobs black men were forced to occupy (street cleaners and garbage cart workers) for high mortality. Infant mortality was linked to the overwork of black women during pregnancy and to the inadequate diets of pregnant and lactating mothers. Butler recommended training more Black physicians and educating the Black masses.[30]

Another report by Georgia Swift King demonstrated that intemperance was a major cause of mortality. She linked alcohol use to disease, crime, and death. Poverty was also listed as a contributing factor in Black mortality. Furthermore, poverty was blamed for producing poor living conditions, poor nutrition, inadequate clothing, and an inability of an individual who was ill to receive good health care. Professor W. B. Matthews reported on the ways in which ignorance caused mortality. He pointed out that city life required more accurate observances of the laws of health than country or village life. He said ignorance made one easy prey for epidemics and contagious diseases. The ignorant violate the rules of health because they do not know them. This study ended by warning against broad generalizations and suggesting further research.

Atlanta University Study no. 2, "Social and Physical Conditions of Negroes in Cities" appeared in 1897. In conducting the research for this study, the investigators were instructed to obtain accurate information without regard to racial pride. Study no. 2 contained data on Black female heads of households and working mothers, as well as provided statistical data in the form of charts on Black Americans in the cities of Atlanta, Baltimore, Charleston, South Carolina, Memphis, and Richmond. The resolutions of this study made specific recommendations for day nurseries, family support, and kindergartens. The recommendations made more than one hundred years ago still are pertinent today.

"Some Efforts of American Negroes for their Own Social Betterment" was Atlanta University Study no. 3. The research focused on black churches, secret societies, and benevolent societies. With this study, Du Bois became the editor. Julius Lester (1971) pointed out that under Du Bois' editorship one of the most important aspects of the studies was the historical framework in which Du Bois presented his subject matter. Du Bois made one of the first attempts to establish a connection between African culture and society and black culture and society in America. Furthermore, he outlined the history of blacks in Africa to show not only the extent and sophistication of African culture, but to show how that culture was modified when blacks were confronted with slavery and Western culture. Through this exposition, Du Bois began to correct the still widely held beliefs that Africa had no culture or civilization worth knowing about.[31] He also began to modify his own bias in reference to European culture.

Robin Law (2007) reassessed the contribution of Du Bois to the development of African historiography and suggested it was a 1906 lecture by Franz Boas at Atlanta University on "The Black Sudan" that piqued his interest and led to his exploration of African history and culture.[32] She posits that prior to the lecture Du Bois had assumed that Africa "had no past" which was the prevailing idea based on information taught in schools throughout the land. However, in 1898 Du Bois clearly is interested in Africa.

Study no. 3 presented the history of several benevolent societies such as Trinity Moral Reform founded in 1850, and the Daughters of Rebecca, 1866. The research showed how these organizations, as well as Black savings banks established in Washington, D.C. in 1888, insurance companies, real estate companies, orphanages, old folks' homes, hospitals, and youth reformatories were instrumental in the betterment of Black life. In the section on the Black church, Du Bois traced its development back to the African roots revealing that the "African clan life of blood relatives became the clan life of the plantation; the religious leader became the head of the religious activity of the slaves, and of whatever group action was left."[33] He went on to show how during the post-slavery era, the minister added political and economic functions to his religious duties. Du Bois' analysis is still apropos of Black ministers today; the Rev. Jesse Jackson, director of Operation P.U.S.H. and candidate for president of the United States in 1984 and 1988, is a prime example.

Atlanta's former mayor, and previous Ambassador to the United Nations, the Rev. Andrew Young is another, as is the Rev. Benjamin Hooks, former national director of the NAACP, not to mention the Rev. Dr. Martin Luther King, Jr. Another contemporary example is the Reverend Al Sharpton. Du Bois concluded the third study, in which he described a total of 236 different organizations, by suggesting that while they were a benefit to society, all Black societies and organizations should do less socializing and more charitable work.

"The Negro in Business" became Study no. 4 of the Atlanta University Studies. Appearing in 1899, this was a scientific survey consisting of extensive tables. Two of the tables were "Negro Business Men by State" and "Negro Business men According to Occupation." The study also included papers presented on Black business ventures in Atlanta, a report by Du Bois on "The Negro Newspaper" that contained historical details on the publication of Black American magazines (3); daily papers (3); weekly papers (136), and school papers (11). Du Bois listed the dates of establishment for all of the papers. This study is now an invaluable source for understanding the roots of Black publications in the United States. The study also provided the "basis for the organization of the Negro Business Men's League developed by Booker T. Washington in 1900."[34]

Study no. 5 was "The College Bred Negro" and appeared in 1900. It consisted of a survey of 2,600 Black college graduates. The questionnaire requested the graduates' biographical and occupational data, political activity, and attitudes. Of the 2,600 questionnaires sent out, 1,252 responses were received. Du Bois summarized and often quoted the responses. Tables included data on entrance requirements for Blacks in college, courses offered, and textbooks used. Additionally, information was included on 390 Black students in white colleges. There were also copies of letters from colleges refusing to admit Black applicants. Du Bois found that among "women's colleges the color prejudice was much stronger and more unyielding."[35]

"The Negro Common School" appeared in 1901 as Atlanta University Study no. 6. It pointed out the gross inadequacy of the system of public education for black people in the South. This study included "A Selected Bibliography of the American Negro for General Readers" which was divided into History, Present Social Conditions, Literature of the American Negro and Other Bibliographical Sources.

"The Negro Artisan" Study no. 7 in the Atlanta University series appeared in 1902. The study included a three-page "Bibliography of the Negro." A questionnaire was sent to Black college graduates and returns came from 32 states, Canada, Costa Rica, and Puerto Rico. A survey of the practice and status of every union affiliated with the A.F. of L. (American Federation of Labor) was also conducted. Of the unions contacted, 97 replied and 11 refused to reply. This study is particularly interesting in that it included quotations from trade union leaders and a letter to Du Bois from Samuel Gompers. Gompers was upset by Du Bois' analysis of racism in the unions.[36]

Study no. 8, appeared in 1903 and focused on the Black American church. It consisted of an historical summary of the impact of religion on Blacks, and vice-versa. Here again, Du Bois made the African connection. The study included information on witchcraft, as well as information on the significance of historic Black spiritual leaders, including Toussaint L' Ouverture, Gabriel Vesey, and Nat Turner. "The Negro Church" concluded with a critique of white Christianity. Du Bois said that when Christians can practice what their religion preached, when they can follow the Golden Rule and the Sermon on the Mount, when "spiritual kinship transcends all other relations" then "the innate wickedness of the human heart" seen in the race problem will be solved.[37]

Published in 1904, "Some Notes on Negro Crime Particularly in Georgia" was Study no. 9 in the series. It alleged that census reports on the subject of Black crime were inaccurate. This study presented a special investigation of court returns and prison data. Study no. 9 also included a three-page "Select Bibliography on Negro Crime." Du Bois concluded that the court system was unfair to Blacks and that social and economic conditions must change before there would be any change in the crime rate.

Study no. 10, "A Select Bibliography of the Negro American," and Study no. 11 "The Health and Physique of the Negro American" were published in 1905 and 1906 respectively. Today Study no. 10 is a one of a kind collection that listed hundreds of magazine articles and pamphlets that are invaluable in Black Studies. This work also contained a bibliography of bibliographies on Black Americans. For Study no. 10, letters were sent to every medical school "of record in the United States" requesting information on the practice of insurance companies, in addition to requesting data on hospitals for Black Americans, medical colleges for Black students, and information on physicians, dentists, and pharmacists. The study also contained valuable quotations from letters to Du Bois, one in fact from Franz Boas. Some of the titles in this study were listed in German and in French.

"Economic Co-operation Among Negro Americans" Study no. 12 posed the question: "How far is there and has there been among Negro Americans a conscious effort at mutual aid in earning a living?"[38] The answer embraced African and West Indian history and referred to conditions of slavery, the underground railroad, aspects of the Civil War and the Reconstruction as conscious and collective Black efforts at mutual aid. Other "types of co-operation" listed included the black church, schools, burial and benevolent societies as well as secret societies, e.g. Masons and Odd Fellows. Du Bois referred to these efforts as group economy, and analyzed all of the organizations for their structure and function. This study provided information that is not contained elsewhere.

Published in 1908, "The Negro American Family" Study no. 13 perhaps is the best known of the Atlanta University Studies. Some of the information contained in the study was used by Daniel P. Moynihan in his study of the so-called "black matriarchy." Du Bois began this study with information on the black family in Africa, then traced the impact of slavery on the family and finally presented the current conditions of the family. Sixteen pages of photographs of African and Black American homes made this study unique. Du Bois emphasized the class differences among Black Americans, something other researchers failed to do. The reports for the 13th study included family budgets, and there is even a copy of a family menu.

Studies no. 14 through 18 were repeats. Du Bois planned to produce a recurring cycle of ten studies in successive decades with repetition of each subject or some modification of it in each decade. His plan resembled the plan that he had developed for the Department of Labor Studies. He wanted to broaden and expand the studies with better methods until they could be called scientific in the broadest sense of the term.[39] Study no. 14, "Efforts for Social Betterment Among Negro Americans," appeared in 1909 and was broadened by its emphasis on the African background and focused on the role of Black women. This data on women's self-help organizations was especially valuable.

Study no. 15, "The College-Bred Negro American," appeared in 1910, and provided information for the 15th Conference entitled "The Higher Education of Negro Americans." The Conference called for more and better high schools and included reports on the experiences of college educated professionals. It contradicted the idea that college education was not helpful to black people.

Study no. 16 was edited with Augustus Dill, Du Bois' former student and successor as teacher of Sociology at Atlanta University. "The Common School and the Negro American," exposed the deterioration in education among Blacks since disfranchisement.

Study no. 17 repeated Study no. 7 on the Black American Artisan. The report further documented racism in the labor movement. "Morals and Manners Among Negro Americans" appeared in 1913 as Study no. 18. By examining official data regarding crime among Blacks and exposing the role of the white press in distorting much of the information about black crime, Du Bois substantiated the findings of this report. When Study no. 18 appeared, Du Bois had already joined the staff of the NAACP and unfortunately his plan for the Studies to continue after his departure from Atlanta University was never realized. He had, however, actually sketched out a design for the studies as follows:

- Population: Distribution and Growth;
- Biology: Health and Physique;
- Socialization: Family, Group and Class;

- Cultural Patterns: Morals and Manners;
- Education;
- Religion and the Church;
- Crime;
- Law and Government;
- Literature and Art; and
- Summary and Bibliography.[40]

Du Bois intended to keep all the inquiries going on simultaneously, emphasizing and reporting on one particular subject as time and development might suggest. His intended plan would thereby allow for adjustments to new scientific advances in fields like anthropology and psychology.[41]

Atlanta University was the only institution in the world carrying on a systematic study of black people and making the results of the study available for scholars of the world.[42] Du Bois had great faith in the role of scholarship as a weapon against ignorance and racism. He assumed white scholars shared his faith. However, he found, as the financial allotment for the studies dwindled, they did not. Of the Atlanta University Studies, Lester (1971) conceded that while the methodology was sometimes inadequate, much was accomplished. With these studies Du Bois countered the generalizations made by whites who sometimes based their facts on observations made from train windows while traveling through the South. Before the Atlanta University Studies it was commonly accepted that Black men were lynched solely because of their alleged proclivity for white women. Du Bois' research showed that in a long series of lynchings, less than one-fourth of the victims had been accused of rape.[43] The Atlanta University Studies were also the first to demonstrate that Black children in the South did not receive the equal education supposedly guaranteed them in the Plessey versus Ferguson decision. Furthermore, Du Bois' work pointed out that black people contributed significantly to the financial support of their own institutions.

The Studies, although limited, incomplete, and only partially conclusive, were so much better than any other investigative attempts of the time; they gained world-wide recognition. In 1900, Du Bois had been able to present to the world much of what had been accomplished by Black Americans. He and various student researchers at Atlanta University put the findings of the Studies into charts and figures which illustrated the size and growth of the Black populous, the age, sex, the distribution, education, occupations, and the books and periodicals written by Blacks. Du Bois took these handmade, color pasteboard charts to the World's Fair in Paris, France. The exhibit received a Grand Prize, and Du Bois was awarded a gold medal.[44]

The Atlanta University Studies totaled 2,172 pages published on the Black American experience. The pages form an encyclopedia for Black Studies today. The studies were widely distributed in the libraries of the world, and according to Du Bois, between 1896 and 1920, there was no study made regarding Black Americans which did not in some way depend on the research carried out by Atlanta University. Nevertheless, the program was not to continue.

Several factors contributed to the demise of the Atlanta University Studies. First, there were insufficient funds to continue the research. Second, Du Bois himself was distracted from the work. In the *Autobiography* he admitted he found it too difficult to remain a detached scientist while black people were being "lynched, murdered and starved"[45] and third, he recognized he had misjudged the demand for the type of work he was doing. He had confidently believed that Americans wanted to be cured of their ignorance regarding black people. He was mistaken. Consequently, Du Bois left Atlanta University for a more politically active career with the NAACP. He saw this move as an opportunity to more directly fight the "real difficulty"—racism and bigotry in America that he was beginning to see were more complex issues than sheer ignorance or stupidity.

The Atlanta University Studies ceased, but the pioneering efforts of Du Bois had produced the first comprehensive scientific studies of Blacks in higher education. This was not, however, the end of Du Bois' contribution to the foundation of Black Studies. He continued to be an advocate for Black Studies, although he failed to call it that. The next section explores Du Bois' ideas for the development of Black Studies.

In "The Conservation of the Races" (1897), an early but significant essay, Du Bois defined race and articulated the importance of the historical component of race in Black Studies. Race is, he contended, "a vast family of human beings, generally of common blood and language, always of common history, traditions and impulse, who are both voluntarily and involuntarily striving together for the accomplishment of certain more or less vividly conceived ideals of life."[46] History was especially important to the study of Black Americans because many historical facts had been distorted and many more simply unknown.

The historical perspective for Du Bois extended all the way back to Africa, providing an aspect missing from most of the current scholarship. There was an aversion to Africa from both Black and white scholars. Apparently this aversion to African origins has not completely disappeared during the ensuing years since Du Bois laid the foundation for Black Studies. Many programs today begin with the study of slavery in America. Du Bois believed "it would be faulty logic to assume that the Negro American can be explained by African origins," but that it was "equally erroneous to assume that black history started during or after slavery."[47] He also argued that "the history of the world is the history, not of individuals, but of groups, not of nations, but of races, and he who ignores it overrides the central thought of all history."[48]

In the "Conservation" essay, Du Bois warned that black people must not be absorbed by white America.[49] He insisted there was a need for black colleges, black publications, black businesses, a black school of literature and art. Perhaps this was the first attempt to establish a black aesthetic. Moreover, he advocated establishing an intellectual clearinghouse for all the products of the Black mind. This last suggestion materialized in March, 1897 as the American Negro Academy. Du Bois hoped that the Academy would help to preserve Black culture and add to the treasure of human accomplishment. Black Americans, as Du Bois saw then, were unique and had a contribution to make to the world based on their collective historical experience in the United States. Du Bois often referred to this experience as psychic history, that is, the historical experience which produced the spirituals or "sorrow songs" as Du Bois called them, and much of what infused the best Black American literature and poetry of the day.

The "Conservation" essay also is interesting for its definition of racial prejudice. Du Bois defined racial prejudice as "the historical friction between different groups of people; the difference in aim, in feeling, in ideals of two different races; if the difference exists touching territory, laws, language, or even religions, it is manifest that these people cannot live in the same territory without fatal collision."[50] In summary, Du Bois' belief in the historical significance of the Black experience in America and the need for scientific and systematic study was clearly stated in the "Conservation." In this essay he also called for maintaining Black American institutions and advocated a black aesthetic. Each of these topics is still relevant to the current issues in Black Studies.

In the 1980s when I first conducted this research, issues regarding a Black aesthetic and the Black Arts Movement were just beginning to wane from their heyday of the late 1960s and early 1970s. Du Bois' definition of race was generally accepted, and there was little objection to the idea of Black essentialism. However, today the idea of an essential aspect of race or blackness is challenged. Scientists know that there is not an essential racial genetic characteristic. Du Bois knew this as well. But were there essential cultural characteristics that he claimed as racial is the question.

In January 1898, "The Study of the Negro Problems" appeared in the *Annals of the American Academy of Political and Social Science.* Du Bois appealed for the scientific study of the Black American experience. He insisted black people deserved study for "the great end of advancing the cause of science in general,"[51] and he pointed out that no such opportunity to watch and measure the history and development of a great race of human beings had ever before presented itself to modern scholars. He reasoned as follows:

> If they dally with the truth to humor the whims
> of the day, they do far more than hurt the good
> name of the American people: they hurt the
> cause of scientific truth the world over, they

> voluntarily decrease human knowledge of a
> universe of which we are ignorant enough, and
> they degrade the high end of truth-seek in a day
> when they need more and more to dwell upon
> its sanctity.[52]

Du Bois presumed Black Studies could also test whether prejudice arose from ignorance or vice versa. More than fifty years would lapse before psychology would attempt a scientific look at prejudice. Gordon Allport's now classic, *The Nature of Prejudice* (1954), grappled with what he called "man's irrational nature."[53] The concept of race, as Du Bois knew, was a recent invention. He even had trouble defining it in "Conservation of the Races" (1897). One reason the race concept became popular is because it provided a visible mark, "by which to designate victims of dislike."[54] Using race as reason and refusing to examine, as Du Bois suggested, the complex issues behind ignorance, poverty, and crime, people accepted the pseudo-scientific biology of race as "irrefutable justification for prejudice."[55] In the 1940s Ashley-Montagu called race "a mischievous and retardative term"[56] and in 1942 published *Man's Most Dangerous Myth: The Fallacy of Race* that stated clearly the only race was the human race. The most appropriate term for culturally cohesive groups would be "ethnic" which is what Du Bois described in "Conservation."

In "The Study of the Negro Problems" essay Du Bois also clarified the problems of Black Americans stating there was not just one unchanging problem. Instead, he said black people faced "a plexus of social problems, some new, some old, some simple, some complex; and these problems have their one bond of unity in the [f]act that they group themselves about those Africans whom two centuries of slavery brought to this land."[57] Du Bois outlined in this essay the theoretical framework and practical means for conducting Black Studies. His overall plan was that Black Studies should include:

> . . . the arrangement and interpretation of historical and statistical matter in light of the experiences of other nations and other ages; it should aim to study those finer manifestations of social life which history can but mention and which statistics can not count, such as the expression of Negro life as found in their hundred newspapers, their considerable literature, their music and folklore.[58]

Du Bois divided the Studies into two categories: first, the study of black people as a special group; and second, the study of the Black American social environment. From these categories Du Bois developed the following four divisions: (1) historical study, (2) statistical investigation, (3) anthropological measurement, (4) sociological interpretation. For Du Bois, Black Studies logically fell under the heading of sociology, but material for historical study, he pointed out, was rich and abundant. For historical research he suggested the use of colonial statutes and records, the archives of Great Britain, France, and Spain, and the collections of historical societies. Statistical investigation, he thought, should tabulate simple matters of numbers, age, sex, and other descriptive facts.[59] Du Bois wanted groups to conduct the statistical studies because he thought they were apt to be more accurate than a general census. Therefore, he pushed for small group samples to cross reference census data.

The third division, anthropological measurement, included the scientific study of the Black physique. The most obvious difference between blacks and whites, Du Bois pointed out, was the physical unlikeness of the two groups. Du Bois wrote that the difference in the physical appearance of Blacks and whites had led to a "mass" of theories—read "mess"—based on flawed scientific evidence. He admitted there are differences, but just what those differences are he insisted no one knew with any scientific accuracy.[60] The bulk of research during this time period forwarded the thesis that black people were different and therefore inferior. The scientific literature reported the brain of black people was "ten percent less in volume and weight"; thus, they from necessity were more under the influence of their instincts and animality than other races of men and less under the influence of their reflective facilities.[61]

The final division, sociological interpretation, mainly dominates Black Studies programs today. This included the arrangement and interpretation of social life, literature, and art. Du Bois concluded that the scope and method of Black Studies needed to be agreed upon beforehand, that is, in terms of the general outline. This, Du Bois said, was "not to hinder the freedom of the individual students but to systematize and unify effort."[62] In laying the groundwork for Black Studies, Du Bois was careful to insist that his students possess a scientific attitude, for he believed science had but one aim: to discover the truth. He frequently said, "The aim of science itself is simple truth."[63] Because of the rigorous standards of scientific detachment, he recognized that several subjects could not be studied "dispassionately and thoroughly." For example, he admitted that no satisfactory study of Black American crime and lynching could be made for a generation or more. Du Bois also maintained that historical and statistical research had but one object, to ascertain facts regarding the social forces and conditions of Black Americans. Only by such a rigid adherence to the true object of the scholar could statesmen and philanthropists of all shades of belief be put into possession of a reliable body of truth which could guide their efforts to the best and largest success.[64]

One recent question that faced Black Studies was under whose jurisdiction it should come. The only proper agencies for conducting Black Studies, according to Du Bois, were the government and the university. The government, he said, could handle the simple, definite inquiries which should be carried out on a broad scale. However, for the more complicated aspects, "where the desideratum is intensive study by trained minds, according to the best methods, the only competent agency is the university."[65] Du Bois went on to say that the very best way for the American university to fulfill its role and to repay its benefactors would be to solve the most vexing social problems,[66] meaning racism, hatred, and discrimination. Du Bois envisioned the historically black colleges and universities in the South as centers of sociological research which would have a close connection and cooperation with Harvard, Columbia, and the best northern and eastern schools.

Another later but extremely influential essay that inspired the growth and development of Black Studies was "Does the Negro Need Separate Schools?" (1936). Without question, Du Bois believed Black Americans needed their own schools and programs of study and development. His position on this issue caused his first break with and subsequent departure from the NAACP. Du Bois saw the proper education of any people as a "sympathetic touch between teacher and pupil . . . not simply of the individual taught, but of his surroundings and background, and the history of his class and group; and contact between pupils, and between teacher and pupil, on the basis of perfect social equality."[67] Obviously, at the time he was writing, these conditions could not be met by the majority of the white institutions. The attitude of whites toward blacks would, Du Bois warned, destroy the teaching and learning atmosphere needed for the black student's success. In this essay he admonished Black American students for failing to possess and/or to value self-knowledge, the kind that could be gained from Black Studies and from attending historically black institutions. He declared:

> As long as the Negro student wishes to graduate from Columbia, not because Columbia is an institution of learning but because it is attended by white students, as long as a Negro student is ashamed to attend Fisk or Howard because these institutions are largely run by black folk, just so long the main problem of Negro education will not be segregation but self-knowledge and self-respect.[68]

As the concept of integration gained acceptance among white Americans, Du Bois apprised Black Americans of the need for Black Studies. It was inconceivable to him for teachers to teach Black students the kind of history they had been taught, say at the University of Chicago. Du Bois advocated black history and sociology and even a black physical science taught by men and women who could understand their audience and who were unafraid of the truth.[69]

When Du Bois first began advocating for Black Studies near the turn of the century, he had thought it was needed for fundamentally different reasons than he later came to realize. In 1935 he admitted:

> There was a time when the ability of Negro brains to do first-class work had to be proven by facts and figures, and I was a part of the movement that sought to set the accomplishments of Negro ability before the world. But the world was a disbelieving world. I did not need the proof for myself. I did not dream that my fellow Negroes needed it; but I have become curiously convinced that until American Negroes believe in their own power and ability they are going to be helpless before the white world, and the white world, realizing this inner paralysis and lack of self-confidence, is going to persist in its insane determination to rule the universe for its own selfish advantage.[70]

Consequently, Du Bois came to realize that Black Studies was necessary for the complete education of black people. He came to believe that Black Americans because of their historical and group experiences, and their psychic memories demanded a certain type of education for the development of self-knowledge and self-confidence.[71] This type of education was not obtainable from the white colleges and universities of the day, as Du Bois acknowledged when he wrote, "Negroes must know the history of the Negro race in America, and this they seldom get in white institutions."[72] Ironically, many did not receive Black history in historically Black colleges or universities either. Far too many were caught in the warp of classical education that took hold in the nineteenth century.

Du Bois provided the guiding principle for Black Studies by continually promoting the idea that students "ought to study intelligently, and from their own point of view, the slave trade, slavery, emancipation, Reconstruction, and present economic development."[73] He believed anthropology, psychology, and the social sciences should be approached from the point of view of the black races. This sounds like the precursor to Afro-centricity. In the "Separate Schools" essay, Du Bois was among the first to promote the idea of celebrating and observing black holidays, something only recently (since the 1960s) being done by Black Americans. Nevertheless, in the 1930s Du Bois was calling for the fifth of March to be commemorated for the martyrdom of Crispus Attucks.

In developing plans for Black Studies, Du Bois carefully guarded against the charge of reverse racism, although the term had not yet been coined. He anticipated the charges and warned that Black American history should "not consist simply of trying to parallel the history of white folk with similar boasting about black and brown folk, but rather (should contain) an honest evaluation of human effort and accomplishment, without color blindness, and without transforming history into a record of dynasties and prodigies."[74] The beginning of many Black Studies programs, unfortunately, did indeed succumb to boasting and the teaching of dynasties and prodigies.

In "The Negro College," which appeared in the *Crisis* in 1933, Du Bois outlined the function of the university. "The university must become not simply a center of knowledge but a center of applied knowledge and guide of action."[75] He meant that the university should serve as an example for the larger society, for he believed colleges and universities were responsible for "great guiding ideals" and group development, that they should expand culture. In his view, the black institutions had not successfully done this, and white institutions had not even made an attempt to recognize black culture, let alone expand, guide, or develop it. Therefore, Du Bois assumed the task lay with Blacks themselves.

In 1933 he wrote that if the college could produce a Black person secure in self-knowledge, who knew how to protect himself and fight race prejudice, "then the world of our dreams will come and not otherwise."[76] He could well have been predicting M.L.K., Jr. or Malcolm X, although one might argue they did not know how to protect themselves, or perhaps there is no protection against American racism and hatred. Nonetheless, Du Bois argued for college teachers to abandon medieval traditions of detached withdrawal from the world. "The professor of mathematics in a college," he said, "has to be more than a counting machine, or proctor of examinations; he must be a living man, acquainted with real human beings, and alive to the relation of his branch of knowledge to the technical problem of living."[77] The educator must be socially conscious and some would argue both conscious and active in addressing social problems.

The teacher in the black college, Du Bois insisted, "had to be something far more than a master of a branch of human knowledge."[78] The faculty of a black college or university, according to Du Bois, needed a social commitment and an awareness of the political world around them. Of course the same is true for Black Studies faculty. One issue, about which some faculty complain, is the value added aspects they are expected to contribute without appropriate recognition or compensation.

In "The Field and Function of the American Negro College" (1933), Du Bois attacked the university for being irrelevant. "The university cut off from its natural roots and from the mass of men becomes a university of the air and does not establish and does not hold the ideal of universal culture which it sought in its earliest days, to make its great guiding end."[79] This essay provided great impetus to the argument for Black Studies and to the efforts to make college education relevant during the late 1960s and early 1970s.

Although Du Bois left his position at Atlanta University to work with the NAACP, he still essayed for the establishment of Black Studies in mainly black colleges and universities; however, his most well planned effort followed his return to Atlanta University in 1934. Du Bois set about to revive the conferences on the Black experience and to publish the studies, but money was scarce, and funds for the conferences were not readily available. Nonetheless, Du Bois was able to obtain funds for a preliminary work in 1940 from the Carnegie Foundation. In April, 1941, Du Bois called the First Phylon Conference. At this Conference he tried to promote his plan for Black Studies. Since Atlanta University did not have the funds to undertake the program, he approached the government supported land-grant colleges.[80] Du Bois argued that the black land-grant colleges would be ideal centers of social studies "on matters touching the condition in each state of the people for whom the school exist [ed] and for whose advancement the school was established."[81] Du Bois believed the Great Depression had exacerbated racial consciousness. The only fundamental way to meet this situation of worsened racial relations was through a serious program of Black Studies. He advocated a program for a total study of the complete situation, continuously photographed, and re-photographed, measured and re-measured that could provide knowledge of the vast and momentous social experiment in race relations taking place in the United States, a program that would attain completeness and authority and be unquestioned, unquestionable and available in the postwar world which would surely need the information.[82] Du Bois saw Black Studies as a way of not only serving black people, but also a unique way of serving the world and social science.

Du Bois planned for three black universities to guide and integrate the work done at the land-grant colleges. Howard University was chosen because of its position with the federal government, Fisk University, because of its well equipped social science department, and Atlanta University because of its experience in being the first institution where Black Studies had been undertaken. Du Bois approached President Banks of Prairie View College which had the best social science department among black land-grant colleges. From Banks Du Bois secured permission to present his plan to the Annual Conference of the Presidents of Negro Land-Grant Colleges. The Conference took place in Chicago in 1941.

In his address to the Conference, Du Bois made two salient points: He pointed out that the federal government was giving $18 million annually to land-grant colleges in the South, and that the black colleges received only about five percent of this money. Requests by the black colleges for a larger share of the funds were denied because research in agriculture or chemistry was being carried out in the white colleges, and it was not deemed necessary to duplicate this work in the black institutions. Du Bois planned, therefore, a careful program of Black Studies as the basis for demanding a fair share of the federal funds.

In his address to the Conference Du Bois admonished the college presidents, saying: "It is not only illogical but it is an indictment of the Negro college that the chief studies of the Negro's condition today are not being done by Negroes in Negro colleges."[83] He insisted that Studies should be brought back under the control of an "Association of colleges, and this not for the purpose of creating a Negro science or purely racial facts, but in order to make sure the whole undistorted picture is there and that the complete interpretation is made by those most competent to do it, through their own lives and training."[84] The argument contained in Du Bois' address to the presidents of the land-grant colleges would be wrestled with in the student-led fight for Black Studies. They would argue for Black professors with real world experience. Finding few to none, they turned to community leaders. Some were admitted to the hallowed halls of learning to teach what they knew of Black life.

Du Bois presented to the Conference of Negro Land-Grant College Presidents an extensive proposal for the implementation of Black Studies. He called for a continuous and intensive study of the black people in each southern state. Du Bois recognized that some of the social science departments in the land-grant colleges were ill-equipped to carry out the scientific study of the Black experience. He, therefore, called for time and funds for research and stated that the departments or divisions of social science should include history, political science, psychology, anthropology, sociology, and economics. Annual conferences were part of the plan for the purpose of discussion, review of the subjects and methods of research so that other college faculty could attend and benefit from the information. Publication of the research was part of the plan.

For each land-grant college Du Bois suggested the division of Social Sciences teach history, anthropology, sociology, economics, psychology, and political sciences. History was to include European, Asian, African, American, meaning the Americas central and south, history of the United States, History of Black People in: Africa, South and Central America and the United States, and in each state. Anthropology should teach social institutions in the modern world, and economics should include systems in the United States and civics and psychology as they related to black people.

Outside of the classroom, studies were to be conducted of the facts concerning black people in each state by counties, subdivisions of counties, villages, towns, cities, wards, blocks and households. The study was to be organized and carried on by professors, instructors, fellows, social workers, volunteers and affiliated organizations. These studies were to include specific information regarding the number of individuals, family groups, character of homes, location of homes, occupation of persons, incomes, expenditures, age, marital relations, education, property, and recreation. Du Bois needed this particular information for a number of reasons. He planned to cross-check the information with that gathered by the Federal census. By scrutinizing the Federal census he hoped to gain any information that might have been missed in either party's research. Having accurate data would enable the studies to do for black people what similar research did for whites.

black people were not the only Americans who were economically poor, uneducated, or who committed crimes and produced children without benefit of marriage. The difference was that among whites the behavior was deemed deviant. For black people it was considered normal. Conclusions were drawn from the abnormal behavior of a minority of black people and then generalized to all black people. If a Black person was well-educated, economically well off, and fit none of the negative statistics surrounding Black behavior, he or she was not seen as an average, hard-working Black person but as an exception to the rule. Du Bois wanted hard facts to counter this sophistic thinking.

The scope of his plan was ambitious and wide ranging. As funds increased, Du Bois wanted the studies to become more intense and comprehensive to include the observation and measurement of all facts and situations which concerned the status of the Black population in each state. He wanted to know virtually every Black family in the state, including their activities, institutions, and organizations, all reports of the State, the county and its subdivisions, concerning education, occupation, dependency and delinquency, all organizations of Blacks working with or for black people and the details of such work, including churches, lodges, cemeteries, clubs, etc., their property and budgets. He intended to gather research on all business conducted by Black and among black people, the kind of business, amount earned, and approximate money value. This information would document the number of commercialized recreations, movies, billiard rooms, gambling, prostitution, etc. as well as count the number of public recreation parks, playgrounds, available to black people. Finally, he intended to ascertain to what extent black people participated in government as voters and officials, taxpayers, and property holders. The methods and scope of these studies would be outlined at the annual conference, with each college represented and would also include outside experts. All the college reports would be brought together, studied, tabulated, analyzed, interpreted and integrated into an annual report. The results would be edited and made public for an annual state meeting and for a public museum and laboratory of the social sciences with maps, charts, and models.

Du Bois planned for the Historically Black private institutions to join with departments of social science in Northern colleges and universities to make similar studies of black people in the North. Eventually, the studies would include black people throughout the nation. The information would not be solely for scholarship but would fulfill a practical purpose as well. It would educate the world about the Black experience and also serve as a tool of social uplift among black people, in addition to serving as a basis of raising the standard of living and cultural pattern of Black Americans through education, work, law, and social action. Du Bois believed remedies existed for every social problem, institutional failure, or individual maladjustment made evident, located, and measured. Organizations would then attempt to discover or promote at the local and state level, remedies in education or other methods for improving the situation. In 1940, when Du Bois set this plan into action, he still believed that the democratic ideal was attainable. His social uplift plan included hiring thoroughly trained social workers, enlisting a corps of volunteers, and advocating for sustained group effort. Social uplift included health care: by physicians and dentists; by group medical care; by hospitalization; by special campaigns against tuberculosis, cancer, heart disease, syphilis, by childbirth and child welfare efforts.

Attention should be paid to recreation including music, a folk theatre, playgrounds, library facilities, and sports. All these efforts, while important would be secondary to the effort to enable black people to earn a living. Du Bois introduced the idea of cooperative economics suggesting that "reorganization, such as is involved in consumers' and producers' cooperation; whereby not only intelligent saving can be made in the expenditure of income, but that new occupations, especially in home industries and small manufacturers, can be established among Negroes."[85] Du Bois' plan for the study of black people was scientific and practical; he intended to include the Black community, not to isolate the people from the conditions they intended to change. He said that "Every attempt should be made to use existing institutions and organizations among Negroes, for undertaking efforts at social reform . . . Churches, fraternal lodges, women's clubs, schools, and in many cases, private businesses, can be used for increasing employment, finding new employment, furnishing legal defense, furnishing direct relief, improving health, organizing recreation, furnishing student aid and promoting consumer, and producer, cooperation."[86]

Du Bois suggested that each college in each state reorganize their budgets in order to provide a gradually increasing minimum of funds for this program. They would need funds to hire and teach the proposed subjects, and for giving trained teachers time and funds for investigation. They would need to hire social workers and fellows for investigation and community outreach. Furthermore, funds were needed for publication of the research. In order to begin the program Du Bois said that they would need one or two history teachers, one or two teachers of anthropology and sociology, one teacher of economics, one teacher of psychology, with laboratory, one teaching fellow with some time and funds for field work, a social worker with time for investigation and advice.[87]

The presidents of the land-grant colleges approved Du Bois' proposal, and on June 12, 1942, they accepted a general plan that would provide for funds to be set aside to establish programs of Black Studies. The plan was signed by the presidents of 20 land-grant colleges, as well as by the presidents of Fisk, Howard, and Atlanta Universities.[88] In addition, it was also endorsed by *School and Society*, the *Journal of Higher Education*, and the *Journal of Negro Education*. Du Bois' plan for the studies was finally implemented on October 28, 1942 and Du Bois was designated the official coordinator of the proposed studies.

On April 19 and 20, 1943, the first conference of the Negro land-grant colleges took place at Morehouse College, in Atlanta, Georgia. A second conference was planned for the spring of 1944. However, in a surprising move by the Board of Trustees of Atlanta University, Du Bois was retired without prior notice. This sudden retirement caused problems for the co-operative venture of the Studies with the land-grant colleges and Atlanta University. As a result, the administration of the program was transferred to Howard University with E. Franklin Frazier, Professor of Sociology and Head of Department, and Consultant in Negro Bibliography at the Library of Congress, in charge. In 1945, an excellent conference was held, but within several years funds were cut and many of the land-grant colleges ceased to cooperate. Eventually the plan failed, at least as Du Bois had conceived it. Nevertheless, his pioneering effort sowed the seeds for the future growth of Black Studies.

CHAPTER 4

A RIVER OF KNOWLEDGE

To be sure, behind the thought lurks the after-
thought . . . . Suppose
— "Of the Training of Black Men," 1903

The problems confronting Black Studies today parallel the issues Du Bois faced. Lack of funding and
inadequate financial support continue to be problems for
some Black Studies programs and departments across the
nation. The struggle for recognition in higher education is
another concern. In the late 1960s during the height of the
struggle for Black Studies to be recognized as a legitimate
area of study in higher education, Martin Kilson, professor
of government at Harvard University and member of the
Harvard faculty committee on African and African American Studies, remarked that advocates of the Black Studies
Movement were inclined to act as if what they had "latched
onto with such fervor was never recognized as worthy or
important until they came along."[1] He went on to point

out that the concept of Black Studies "stands squarely on the shoulders of other men—black and white—who have long been concerned with the systematic and honest study of the Negro in American history and society."[2] Failure to recognize the pioneers of the Black Studies Movement resulted in a variety of problems.

Kilson suggested that had proper attention been paid to the contributions of certain notable black scholars, many of the concerns raised about academic validity, subject matter content, and scholarship might have been put to rest. He named in particular professor and historian Carter G. Woodson, a graduate from the University of Chicago and a Harvard Ph.D., who aided in the foundation of the Study of Negro Life and History, and who edited *The Journal of Negro History*, the official publication of the organization; and the contributions of E. Franklin Frazier, a sociologist trained at the University of Chicago, whose book *The Negro in the United States* (1948) ranked among the best of social history books; plus the contributions of St. Clair Drake, whose *Black Metropolis* (1945) was a landmark in urban sociology; as well as professor Horace Mann Bond, author of *The Education of the Negro in Alabama—A Study in Cotton and Steel* (1937), a classic in the sociology of education; the works of Melville Herskovits, and the scholarship of the American Council of Learned Societies "Committee on Negro Studies" (1941–1950), not to mention the pioneering efforts of Du Bois.

Instead, student activists and some faculty sought to project the Black Studies Movement as something new, failing to recognize the academy's ingrained resistance to any new ideas.[3] Herein lies the paradox. Many young people advocating for Black Studies had never heard of the black scholars mentioned above, ergo, the need for

Black Studies. The history of the struggle for recognition in higher education dates as far back as Du Bois' Department of Labor Reports and his study and publication of *The Philadelphia Negro* (1899) and continues throughout the years of the Atlanta University Studies.

In the 1960s the movement gained massive support from black and white students and community folk.[4] Not surprisingly the movement would begin in California where the lack of historically black colleges and universities (HBCUs) existed. West coast black and white students had for the most part missed the Civil Rights revolution led by students in the South. Those students who did participate in the Student Nonviolent Coordinating Committee (SNCC) activities during the summer politicized students who had not been involved but who had watched the events unfold on the nightly news. The climate was disposed for transformation. The 1964 Free Speech Movement at the University of California, Berkeley, the Anti-War Movement led by Students for a Democratic Society (SDS) raised the social and political consciousness of hundreds of white college and university students. SNCC and the Black Power Movement led to black student awareness of the miseducation they were receiving.

San Francisco State College (now university) was the site of student demands and uprisings. The timing was perfect. Unlike the prim and proper coeds that Du Bois chastised for focusing on Greek organizations and wearing fur coats,[5] these students were working class, of diverse ethnicities, with strong ties to the surrounding communities; moreover, they were socially aware and politically engaged. When the students joined forces and the black community backed them, the movement became both powerful and successful.

On February 9, 1968, Nathan Hare became the director for the embryonic Black Studies department.[6] All did not proceed smoothly, and because of administrative delays and balking by the Board of Trustees in implementing the proposal that Hare presented, students called a strike on November 6, 1968.[7] Students shut the campus down, and while at the time it appeared they were more active and powerful than students had ever been, such is not the case. In 1921 Fisk students protested and forced the resignation of their white president. Angry students at Hampton University in 1927 called a strike against the white administration. Their anger and indignation spread to Fisk University in Nashville, Tennessee, Howard University in Washington, D.C., Lincoln University in Pennsylvania, Shaw University in Raleigh, North Carolina, and Johnson C. Smith in Charlotte, North Carolina. An angry Hampton student wrote to Du Bois stating: "The future of the Negro youth depends upon the results of this serious uprising."[8] San Francisco State College students forced the first institution in higher education to establish a Black Studies department and thus established the paradigm for students across the nation. For example, in 1969 black students at Cornell demanded Black Studies. When the administration rejected the students' demands, their protest shut the campus down.[9] One single striking difference in these late twentieth-century black student uprisings was community support.

Turner (1980) offers the most thorough analysis of the development of Black Studies prior to the 1960s, although he omits the contribution to the roots of Black Studies made by Du Bois and identifies instead the period between 1913 and 1929 as the time when the foundation of Black Studies was laid. Turner does, however, state that

"Du Bois launched Black Studies institutionally when he became the director of the Atlanta University Studies Series, which documented social and economic analyses of all aspects of Black American life."[10] Turner identifies the decade of 1930–1940 as a period when Black Studies emerged as a field of study. More voices were added to those of Du Bois and Carter G. Woodson. In 1933 Joseph J. Rhoads, president of Bishop College, called for Black Studies to be included in the college curriculum; and in 1936 Lawrence Reddick joined the push for the scientific study of the black experience.[11] In 1928, Tuskegee Institute offered two courses in Black Studies: The Negro in America and Minority Group Problems were both taught by the Department of Sociology.[12]

As the results of the Great Depression became widespread, Black Studies was affected; for while the idea did not disappear completely, the issue faded from widespread debate.[13] Nevertheless, in 1938 a coalition of black social scientists inaugurated the Howard University Studies in the social sciences to complement the previously published series in history. This was a contribution to the survival of Black Studies; however, it was not enough to amount to a fully developed Black Studies program. One of the complaints of students in the 1960s was that black institutions were not black enough. Amiri Yasin Al-Hadid recognizes the irony that the first Black Studies department is established at San Francisco State instead of at an historically black college or university (HBCU). Nor should the paradox go unnoticed that Hare, a former Howard University faculty in sociology who worked with students to make the Howard curriculum "relevant to the black experience," is the one to establish the first department.[14] The problem with HBCUs was clear to Hare, who observed that, "The Negro college is glued to the mores of its missionary origins."[15] Maulana Karenga responded to the question of how central Black Studies is to the mission of historically black colleges when he said, "The black colleges have a checkered record. In fact, one of the problems we had when we were establishing Black Studies,[sic] was the traditional black colleges, who [sic] assumed that being black and knowing black were the same thing. They confused ontology with epistemology and weren't aware of it."[16] Too many were fearful of following their own path and thus imitated the curricula of white institutions.

By the 1930s the conception of the form that Black Studies should take as an academic field had been developed, but the theoretical delineation of the salient research tasks had not been solidified. There was not as yet the consistent social theory necessary to concretize and unify black inquiry.[17] World War II dampened the theory-building efforts, and by 1940 the emphasis in Black Studies had shifted. Black scholars in history and the social sciences began to create a radical perspective in Black Studies.[18] The publication of Du Bois' *Black Reconstruction in America* (1935) and other seminal works by black authors forced the recognition of a new interpretation of the status of black Americans and their past. By the end of the 1930s, Black Studies began to assume its present form.[19] That form, I suggest, owes its foundation to the efforts Du Bois made with the black land-grant colleges.

From 1940 to 1960 the cold war, McCarthyism, and the anti-intellectual attitude of the times combined to create a period of intellectual hiatus for Black Studies, although some scholarly efforts continued. In 1941, for example, historian Waldo Leland attempted to define Black Studies or "Negro Studies" as it was called during this period. He said Negro Studies was "the effect . . . upon American culture of the transfer of African cultures and civilization to a new world where, in a new physical, social, and human environment, they have had a part in producing what we now call American Civilization."[20] Leland demanded that American scholarship no longer concentrate exclusively on Western civilization, but that it broaden its base to include world culture. During this period the American Council of Learned Societies' Committee on Negro Studies succeeded in microfilming black American newspapers printed prior to 1900, drafted a roster of scholars working in "Negro Studies," and published a guide in the national archives of materials on the Black American.[21] This was also the time during which Du Bois introduced his program to the black land-grant colleges. When that program failed, there was not a resurgence of the intellectual validity of Black Studies until the 1960s.

During the early 1960s economic growth and prosperity, as well as the dynamic force of the Civil Rights Movement, produced a mood in the United States that was less constrained. There was even a sense of urgency to protect the democratic rights of dissent and to honor self-expression. This environment rejuvenated independent intellectual discourse in colleges and universities.

The latter part of the 1960s was fraught with student strikes against the general malaise of the status quo, a common affliction in all levels of American education; but these strikes spread nationwide. Turner (1980) points out that black students raised the most potent issues about the form and content of higher education. The quest for Black Studies in American higher education created, according to Turner, "the most poignant intellectual crisis"[21] in history. Part of the reason for such student demands was that the doors of opportunity had swung open in response to civil rights legislation, the Black Power Movement, the assassinations of Malcolm X, King, and Kennedy. Martin Luther King, Jr. scholarships were set aside for black students and admissions and financial aid granted to inner-city students who could not have gained admissions a decade earlier. These students were not interested in assimilating into the culture of white America. They had no desire to become black Anglo-Saxons.

The issues surrounding Black Studies were analyzed and discussed with greater intensity and with more attention from the national media, in faculty committee reports, in professional journals, and in speeches than any other academic issue in the recent history of American higher education. Yet, too few recognized the long and varied history of the struggle for Black Studies intellectual discourse in higher education.

While the time and intensity of efforts for the recognition and acceptance of Black Studies as an intellectually valid interdisciplinary field of study took place in the 1970s, there were major problems to be faced and overcome by the advocates of these studies.[22] One major problem was that Black Studies was intimately related to contemporary problems and issues that could not be discussed purely in the abstract.[23] This characteristic unwittingly thrust Black Studies into the realm of politics. This singular issue sparked long and heated debates.[24] Those upset by the polemics inherent in Black Studies insisted that education and higher learning should be kept separate from politics and ideology.[25] Many students and some scholars condemned the claim of neutrality as a sham and insisted that science demanded truth, not neutrality, a point made by Du Bois over half a century earlier.[26] They recognized, as had Du Bois, that racism made neutrality in studying the black experience an impossibility.[27] Opponents of neutrality[28] readily admitted that all groups of people, academicians included, were influenced in their work by their position in society. To them scholarship had been and still was political, and "the separation between knowledge and politics is artificial and based on a contrived myth about 'value- free' knowledge."[29] Lange (1983) called the objection to politics a desire for "objectivity of the impossible (i.e., that social scientists think, talk, and write as if they were independent of history, culture, and society.)"[30] Gates (2006) admits that the idea of a completely value-free scholarship is "elusive," at the same time he thinks that it is desirable. On the other hand, he calls for the acceptance of both intellectual and political pluralism.

Nevertheless, Black Studies represented an effort to reunite knowledge and politics. The influence from the activities and results of science and scholarship were politically significant, the opponents of neutrality argued. The "pretense toward neutrality by mainstream scholarship," Turner wrote, "is the source of its large failure and discredit; and it is to the enduring credit of Black Studies that it is more candid about this question."[31] Still other scholars insisted that once the door was opened political bias would distort and undermine scholarship.[32] Some, who thought American scholarship was already biased, distorted, and undermined by racism in all its various forms, said it was not a question of politics but rather whose politics?[33] Both Karenga and Allen explained that the university was a political institution. Allen defined the function of the university as the political servant of the bourgeois order, one that prepares academic and professional elite to manage America on behalf of the white power-holding classes. The university is not apolitical and to call for the "depoliticizing" of Black Studies only obscures and confuses the issue.[34]

The question of politics and scholarship as strange bedfellows raged on, and surrounding this issue were concrete and difficult problems to be solved. Some students and scholars wanted Black Studies to emphasize black community involvement,[35] which was controversial. Students accused many faculty and administrators of "ivory-tower-ism," that is, being safe in their ivory tower of academia, for some academics were reluctant to deal with the real problems inherent in the political issues of the black community.[36] Those who argued against community involvement claimed it belonged more properly to schools of social work.[37] Du Bois' position on this issue was that Black Studies should provide the theoretical framework from which the schools of social work could practice;[38] however few, during the heat of argument, were consulting the works of Du Bois.

The problem of politics in Black Studies was further complicated by groups that wanted to push a particular ideological point of view. These groups believed knowledge represented power that often served an ideological function.[39] On the other hand, those in opposition criticized the attempt to establish theoretical underpinnings for Black Studies.[40] Black cultural nationalists, led by M. Ron Karenga (1969), espoused the belief that education was not an "academic thing." It was, Karenga argued, "basically a political thing, and it provides identity, purpose, and direction within an American context."[41] It would follow then, according to the logic of cultural nationalists, that education should do this very same thing for Black American students.

Other scholars[42] argued that Karenga's theory implied an endorsement of the two-nation theory or black nationalism. In general the academic community was opposed to the idea of black nationalism. Several scholars attempted to calm the hysteria Karenga and his group of cultural nationalists incited. Cruse (1969) explained that cultural nationalism is nothing but the attempt of a group or nation or minority to express what is indigenous to its own historical background in order to enhance its public image—social image—in the eyes of the world. Cultural nationalism is nothing but an attempt to prevent the cultural particularism of the dominant white group from continuing to overshadow and submerge the essence of the black experience in America.[43]

Cruse reasoned that cultural nationalists existed because of the failure of integration. Redkey (1969) clarified this concept further in his outline of the three basic patterns of acculturation. He described (1) Anglo-Assimilation, which assumes that to become a proper American one must adopt the prevailing Anglo-American forms and standards of life; (2) the melting pot, where each ethnic group, each group of migrants, people from each section of the country, contribute their own unique qualities to the standard American culture, and where in the end we are a homogeneous American blend; and (3) cultural pluralism or subcultures within American society that have their own values, their own aesthetics, and their own traditions. Black cultural nationalists, he concluded, emerged from number three.

Despite the simplification these scholars tried to impose on the nationalist movement, there were various brands of nationalism that continued to problematize the issues. For example, some nationalists wanted Black Studies to serve as a training ground for black revolutionaries.[44] Still others wanted to train community leaders.[45] There were religious nationalists—members of the Nation of Islam, also known as Black Muslims; and there were economic nationalists, called black capitalists. Turner (1973) defined still another aspect of nationalist philosophy that embraced the belief that "all things created and occupied by blacks should be controlled by black people, and that the purpose of every effort should be toward achieving self-determination . . . and a relatively self-sufficient Black community."[46] This concept produced a variety of approaches to reach the desired goal. Black students wanted and often demanded control of their own programs.[47] Others wanted to exclude whites from teaching courses and/or from taking classes in Black Studies.[48] The demand for separate, autonomous programs run entirely by Blacks caused as much strife as the issue of politics. Those who opposed autonomous and all black programs[49] argued that whites needed to be educated about black Americans' experience in United States.

Advocates of Black Studies as strictly an educational program for the dissemination of knowledge and the promotion of scholarship were appalled at the effort to limit the promulgation of that knowledge.[50] Supporters of the separatist idea claimed that whites in Black Studies classes would retard and otherwise inhibit free and open discussion.[51] Additionally, they believed that few if any whites were qualified to teach the black experience.[52] Some Black scholars supported this aspect of the separatist issue because of their beliefs that teaching Black Studies required a cultural sensibility—i.e., social and aesthetic values, politics, subject content relevant to the varied sensibilities of the students.[53]

Du Bois had expressed the similar concern in the essay "Does the Negro Need Separate Schools?" (1935) when he stated: "Race prejudice in the United States is such that most Negroes cannot receive proper education in white institutions."[54] Du Bois further claimed that Harvard, Yale, and Columbia admit black students, but they are not welcomed; and at Princeton they cannot even enroll. There is but little doubt that many black people believed that what was true in 1935 was still characteristic of higher education at the beginning of the student-led Black Studies Movement. The qualities needed to teach black students Black Studies were found to be lacking in their white colleagues, and indeed missing from American scholarship with regard to Black life and history. Richard Long in "Black Studies: Year One" (1969), pointed to the kind of studies that had been conducted by whites on black people that led to the "culturally deprived" thesis and pathology theory. Further, Long discussed the imperialistic approach to Black Studies. One example that he offered was the case of Mary Washington College in Fredericksburg, Virginia, which had no record of enrolling black students or of hiring black faculty. They decided to become the experts on blacks by establishing a Black Studies Journal. Long commented on the arrogance and academic ill manners of such an attempt. Academic imperialism was linked to capitalist materialism that prompted many people motivated by greed to jump on the Black Studies band wagon and flood schools and colleges with inauthentic Black Studies products for profit.[55]

Butler (1981) wrote that "the process of education and learning is inextricably linked to cultural and basic sensibilities."[56] As a result of the black experience in America, blacks are, according to Butler, likely to have a different sensibility. Turner (1980) recalled that as early as 1913 Du Bois recognized that the development of what is now Black Studies could not be done by anyone other than by trained black scholars.

Aside from the alleged inability of the white academic to correctly interpret the black experience, and because of the lack of knowledge and sensitivity regarding black life, culture, and history in American higher education, many black scholars demanded autonomous programs.[57] Some remembered past experiences, and on the basis of these previously learned lessons, decided in favor of separate programs. The experiences of the Civil Rights Movement had demonstrated to some black Americans that whites could not be helpful unless they were in charge.[58] This take-charge attitude on the part of liberal whites had caused the rift in the Civil Rights Movement and precipitated the cry for "Black Power!"[59] Long identified white behavior as paternalism, the kind that would grant money in order to control the direction and activities of Black Studies. The following event was a case in point. Harris (1982) recalled that the Conference on Negro Studies held at Howard University on March 29 and 30, 1940, was well funded by Carnegie money. The conference, prompted by the action of the Carnegie Corporation in 1937, invited Gunnar Myrdal, a Swedish economist, to conduct a comprehensive investigation of blacks.[60] That Du Bois was passed over, as well as other capable black scholars for this important task, was proof enough for some that whites could not be fair nor could they be trusted to work in the best interests of blacks. They relegated black scholars who were included in this project to the level of research assistant, and some of the most valuable monographs by these social scientists never were published nor cited by Myrdal.[61] Nevertheless, there were black scholars who continued to hope that with the aid of white scholars they could further the goals of black scholarship. Thus, in 1940 when Melville Herskovits approached Ralph Bunche to request the use of Bunche's offices at Howard University for the conference, Bunche complied with the request even though he was not invited to join the Committee on Negro Studies.[62]

The black scholars who attended the conference wanted to address segregation and scholarship. They were concerned about the problems black scholars faced when trying to conduct research, particularly in the South, where they were barred from and denied complete access to libraries and historical societies. Herskovits was described as responding as a "detached intellectual, not an activist."[63] Consequently, under his leadership no action was taken, racism in scholarship continued, which subsequently caused Du Bois to resign from the AAUP (American Association of University Professors) in 1945. His resignation was a form of protest against racism, for meetings were held in places that excluded black members.[64] On the basis of these and many other historical facts of discrimination, some black American scholars refused to entrust the success of Black Studies programs to white administrators or faculty.[65]

Academicians who opposed Black Studies in general and separate programs in particular insisted that those who wanted all-black environments should go to black colleges and universities.[66] Furthermore, Riesman and Jencks (1967) charged that even in black schools the majority of blacks were not really interested in Black Studies.[67] Cruse (1969) pointed out that the emphasis of black colleges and universities had been to educate for social status. However, aside from the pioneering work at Atlanta University, Nick

Aaron Ford (1973) conducted a survey that documented the extent to which black institutions supported Black Studies before it became popular to do so.

Fisk University, for example, offered courses as early as 1921. A total of forty-two courses were offered before the 1967 student revolution. Among the courses offered in 1921–22 were "Music 113, The Study of Negro Music; and Sociology 124, Problems of Negro Life Social Service Training Course (class work and field work)."[68] In 1925–26 the first course in black literature appeared, followed by history, anthropology, religion, and the Negro church. To those courses already being offered, Fisk responded with forty-three new courses between 1967 and 1971.[69] The study revealed similar trends at other black schools, including the findings reported by McClendon (1974).

Therefore, while "black colleges aped white institutions in many respects and even failed to devote sufficient time in a formal manner to the many aspects of the black experience in America and in the world,"[70] they did not graduate students without exposing them to some aspects of the black experience. This is more than could be said for white institutions. In the 1960s Ford correctly pointed out that a student could complete an elementary, secondary, college and university education in the United States without ever enrolling in a single class in black social science, humanities, fine arts, or having a single black teacher. Such an occurrence is still possible today.

The difficulty students and faculty faced trying to establish Black Studies in higher education was intensified by unclear objectives and hard to measure outcomes. Objectives for various programs were wide ranging and diverse. Newton (1975) compared the objectives of Black Studies at Western Illinois University and Northeastern

Illinois State College and found they were representative of the widely differing objectives in the field.[71] At the university the stated objectives were to:

1. Demolish the fallacies, myths, and distortions pertaining to history, culture, and life styles of black Americans;
2. Recognize and illuminate the contributions of black people to world civilization and most especially to American heritage;
3. Investigate, explore, and define the black experience;
4. Provide an organized body of knowledge for systematic study.

At the state college in Chicago he found the stated objectives were to:

1. Fit its resources to the total community problem;
2. Liberate its community in mind and then in concrete experiences;
3. Touch base with all disadvantaged groups in the city;
4. Serve as an invaluable resource and natural base as a multiethnic university complex.

For those desiring a more cohesive set of goals, the issue of diversity in stated objectives caused problems. Williams (1981) called for "a clear distinction . . . between Black Studies as an academic discipline and as a social answer to pressing problems."[72] For others, however, the freedom to adapt objectives to local needs was preferred.

To be sure, there were other problems to face and over-come before Black Studies in higher education would be recognized as a legitimate area for undergraduate and graduate study. The aforementioned problems were by far the most serious. Other concerns were generally dismissed as superficial or pseudo concerns voiced in order to obstruct the development of various Black Studies programs. Questions regarding the employability of persons with degrees in Black Studies were answered by those whose reasoning was akin to Du Bois when he said:

> The function of the university is not simply to teach bread-winning, or to furnish teachers for the public schools, or to be a center for polite society; it is above all to be the organ of that fine adjustment between real life and the growing knowledge of life, an adjustment which forms the secret of civilization.[73]

Advocates for the programs reasoned that a degree in Black Studies was as marketable as one in philosophy or classics, and no one questioned whether or not these should be a part of higher education. Chemistry professor, Carol Taylor (1981) suggested that these kinds of questions arose from the indifference or reluctance to learn about or to teach the black experience. Questions became less significant, however, as large numbers of colleges and universities began to institute programs in Black Studies. In April 1969, the Black Studies program at Harvard University was granted departmental status[74]; the W.E.B. Du Bois Institute for Black Research also began as the research arm for the Black Studies department, accepting pre- and postdoctoral research fellows. In 1969 Boston University began offering a graduate degree in Black Studies, making it the oldest graduate program in the United States.[75] Thus, it could be said that Black Studies had finally gained a measure of recognition in higher education. Perhaps even more significant than these northeastern institutions, Emory University in Atlanta, Georgia, instituted an African and African American Studies program in 1971, the first of its kind in the Deep South at a white institution, and it was headed by a black woman with a Ph.D. in sociology who directed the program for twenty years.[76]

While some programs fell by the wayside because of budget constraints and insincere commitments from administrators, the program at Harvard remained viable with enrollments of between 30 to 100 students, black, white, Hispanic and Asian.[77] The program at Boston University is still functional; however, it is enervated by declining student enrollment.[78] In spite of the proliferation of Black Studies programs, concerns about intellectual excellence and the refusal of the academic establishment to recognize the scholarship of Black Studies amounted to a serious problem, one that challenged the academic and intellectual integrity of black students and scholars.[79] However, genuine concerns for academic and intellectual excellence often were mistaken for racist efforts to attack the programs.[80]

In an effort to elucidate the intellectual and political issues connected with Black Studies, in 1969, Yale University held a conference, entitled Black Studies in the University, where many voiced their concerns. The questions and issues raised at the Yale conference were reflections of apprehensions that existed throughout the academic community. Because Black Studies was in demand, some educators questioned the moral responsibility involved in complying with public pressures for curriculum reforms.[81]

Other educators seriously challenged the assertion that the experience of black people in Africa and in the new world was a subject of sufficient amplitude and depth to justify general study and instruction in higher education.[82] Others asked whether or not the "special" study of Black Americans was intellectually valid and socially constructive for both black and white students. Taylor (1969) questioned the intellectual significance of focusing a part of the curriculum consciously and directly on the Black experience. Was race a proper organizing principle for the curriculum? Answers came from both students and scholars affirming the appropriateness of Black Studies. Taylor (1969) himself pointed out that geographical, national, religious, and ethnic distinctions were used in the organization of curriculum and in the attack upon intellectual problems, but not race. He asked if this omission was educationally responsible.

Delores Aldridge (2000) founding director of the Black Studies program at Emory University recalled that by the 1970s many programs "were being characterized as 'feel-good studies.' The curriculum was being characterized as ideological brain washing. The pedagogy was thought to be unstructured 'rap sessions' and many of the faculty were judged unqualified to teach in higher education."[83] In order to counter the spread of misperception at best and specious slander at worst, Black Studies advocates in 1975 formed a professional organization, the National Council for Black Studies (NCBS). The organization would support professional development and standardized curricula and would centralize program data.[84]

As for the validity of the Black experience, Gerald McWorter (1969) (aka Abdul Alkalimat) stated: "If any human experience is relevant for intellectual consideration—the black experience has to be included."[85] Kilson (1969) observed that colleges and universities study the social structures of lower-class black American families because they constitute and represent certain kinds of problems that the society can no longer ignore. He said, "When somehow and in some way there is a relative consensus that the bloody thing is a problem, it automatically gets intellectual validity."[86] Some scholars argued that the university as an institution had developed blind spots, and that this should be remedied. There was, they believed, intellectual integrity in further widening the range of inquiry and the range of discussion in looking at new problems.[87] Taylor (1969) was convinced it was of grave academic importance to recognize the large range of material that had been ignored in higher education. This ignorance, he maintained, was at least as detrimental to whites as to blacks and, therefore, should be remedied in all segments of academic society and the society at large. Some sought to acknowledge the intellectual debt to those scholars who, although largely ignored, were studying and documenting black American culture long before it became in vogue to do so.[88]

C.H. Taylor pointed out that Black Studies was socially constructive for blacks and whites when he declared, and it is worth quoting, that

> Black students' protest is not simply . . . their proper demand to know more about themselves, about their heritage and their tradition, but rather their consciousness of how important it is for American Society, for the white majority, to know a lot more about them. We need this knowledge to attack not only conscious prejudice, which is easy to identify, but

to overcome unconscious discrimination, that simple lack of awareness, the ignorance from which we all suffer in white America.[89]

Wright (1970) concluded that without Black Studies neither black nor white students would truly be educated. Another concern regarded the lack of subject matter for teaching Black Studies.[90] The interdisciplinarity of Black Studies also posed problems for those academics for whom an interdisciplinary approach represented "watered-down" and less than excellent ways of teaching and learning.[91] Still other issues focused on the lack of resources available for excellent academic programs. Both Bundy[92] (1969) and McWorter (1969) pointed to the shortage of instruments of teaching (i.e., out-of-print books), bibliographic and library tools, and above all, trained and qualified instructors. Still other worries centered on what students often called "programmed failure," that is, when administrators were selected who were not sufficiently qualified to ensure the success of the program.[93] This pattern also applied to the selection of students that entered Black Studies programs. Oftentimes the students were ill prepared for college work and would not have been accepted at the college or university except into the Black Studies department. If and when these students failed or dropped out, a shadow would be cast upon the program. But sometimes the students passed, when they should have failed, and this cast further doubt on the academic integrity of the program.[94]

Many academics were dissatisfied because there was no clearly articulated philosophy of Black Studies.[95] Within the muddle of all the various attempts to articulate the philosophy of Black Studies, Du Bois' statement remains the most apropos. At the turn of the century he proclaimed the double consciousness in being both black and American. In 1903 he said that black people were "born with a veil" into an American world that yields blacks no "true self-consciousness, but only lets him see himself through the revelation of the other."[96] Certainly this was the truth for black students in white colleges and universities. Students who demanded Black Studies were seeking that "self-conscious" personhood that Du Bois referred to in describing double consciousness. Most black students did not wish to "Africanize America" but neither did they intend to bleach their black "soul in a flood of white Americanism."[97] Their effort was to be both black and American and to know as much about their black heritage as they had been forced to learn about the American one that excluded them on the basis of their skin color.

The Du Boisian idea of double consciousness is problematic for some who understand it as an effort to include Africa in the black American experience.[98] Sociologist Alford Young (2006) argues that embedded in Du Bois' use of the term is a reference to "African consciousness that consisted of spirituality," juxtaposed with American materialism. The problem, as Young sees it, is that the average black person at the turn of the century had neither the time nor the desire to contemplate the consciousness of either Africa or America. He reasons that there is no memory of Africa to produce internal conflict. Young writes that "[T]he problem remains in that only African Americans who share [Du Bois'] privileged status are positioned to entertain esoteric thoughts about whatever may be some essence or foundation of blackness, and it is the entertaining of such thoughts that is a precursor to the emergence of a double consciousness."[99] His assumption that only the elite contemplate blackness boggles the mind.

The conundrum of identity in the United States certainly is not based on class. One need only recall the question posed by Malcolm X: What do you call a black man with a Ph.D.? A nigger was the answer. Malcolm also argued that just because kittens were born in an oven, they did not become biscuits. And he directed his arguments to the ordinary working-class, unemployed, or imprisoned black person. I would argue that double consciousness is part of being black in the United States. One does not have to be educated in order to feel the "twoness." The experience of being in America but not of America is not class based. The oven experience of America to which Malcolm X refers does not change Africans into Americans, as he argues; however, it does render a change. Kittens born in an oven, especially if the heat is on, are different from those born in natural surroundings. The street corner conversations of black men in the United States as well as the folklore of black women and men make it clear that they do in fact contemplate double consciousness, although they might not articulate it as eloquently as a Du Bois.

Using Du Bois' philosophy of double consciousness, which she claims represents the mystique in Black Studies, Professor of American Ethnic Studies Johnella Butler (1981) identified two other problems related to curriculum. She asked these provocative questions: How do identity and sensibility function within a curriculum? And how do the problems of combining the ideational and operative aspects of the curriculum, and the structure of departments, allow for this combining? Butler attempted to solve these problems by employing Frye's (1976) theoretical curriculum model. Identity and sensibility function within Frye's curriculum on three different levels, i.e., examination, celebration, and reflection. Examination includes the history, anthropology, political science, economics, and sociology. Celebration, which is subjective and intuitive, embodies black sensibility in music, literature, film, dance, theatre, and folklore, and reflection includes psychology, philosophy, and religion.[100]

Finally, there was the need to clearly define Black Studies. Definitions abound, but few matched the definition articulated by Butler (1981), who defined it as:

> an interdisciplinary field of study focusing on the cultural, that is, cosmological, artistic, historical, social, political, and economic realities of the Black American and American experiences in the United States as they interact with and confront one another.[101]

Concern over academic and intellectual excellence in Black Studies has not ceased. The issue of Black epistemology is still called into question. In 2000, Russell Adams critiqued the ongoing questioning of black knowledge and truth seeking, citing the *Chronicle of Higher Education* article "Why Colleges and Students Need Black Studies" as an answer to the on-going challenge. Turner (1980) believed that Black Studies in higher education had produced some excellent academic programs, and that the studies were likely to remain a part of higher education, in one form or another, whether in the form of several courses or as a department offering a broad range of subjects. Work is being carried on by the National Council on Black Studies in order to surmount its current status. Ethnocentrism versus racism was and still is but another distraction from the legitimacy of Black Studies. The usual euphemism is "reverse racism." The charge was aimed at programs that sought autonomy and/or to exclude or limit white participation in Black Studies.[102] "Black racist" was voiced repeatedly in outcries against quotas, against affirmative action, and against the exclusion of whites from many aspects of Black Studies.[103] In regard to this charge some scholars[104] concluded with Thelwell (1980), who said:

> The black experience in this country is not merely one of political and cultural oppression, economic exploitation, and the expropriation of history. It also includes the psychological and intellectual manipulation and control of blacks by the dominant majority. The liberation of blacks requires, therefore, the redress of all these depredations.[105]

Liberation could not be achieved by whites controlling the situations that they had created and maintained for their own benefit.

Other scholars who resented the charge of "reverse racism" attempted to demonstrate through their analysis of racism that it would be difficult indeed for Black Studies programs to practice it. Jones (1972) distinguished between racism and prejudice, stating that prejudice was a negative attitude toward a person or group based upon a social comparison process in which the individual's own group was taken as the positive point of reference. The Black Studies programs, as well as many other programs, were probably composed of people who were prejudiced.[106] On the other hand, as Jones explained, racism, while quite similar, was distinguished by its power—power that the in-group has over an out-group. In this case the power of whites over blacks.

Racism operates on several levels, the first being the individual. Individual racism is the closest to race prejudice.[107] Racism includes a belief in the superiority of one's own race over another and the behavioral enactments that maintain those superior and inferior positions. Since blacks were clearly in an inferior position, it followed that their behavior was not intended to maintain the status quo, but neither was it to reverse positions.[108] Prejudice, as opposed to racism, may be passive; while racism is active.

Carmichael and Hamilton (1967) described another aspect of racism as institutional. Institutional racism appears in two forms. The first is the "extension of individual racist beliefs; this consists primarily of using and manipulating duly constituted institutions so as to maintain a racist advantage over others."[109] Examples they used included the grandfather clause (if your grandfather could not or did not vote, neither could you), and the poll taxes. The second brand of institutional racism is the by-product of certain institutional practices that operate to restrict on a racial basis the choices, rights, mobility, and access of groups of individuals. While these unequal consequences may be unintended, they are none the less real. Examples of institutional racism might include situations where an advantage was given to all applicants who had studied abroad. Without identifying blacks, they would nonetheless be excluded due to the fact that only a small number of blacks might have had the means to study abroad.

Jones (1972) described still another form of racism he referred to as cultural. Cultural racism advocates the superiority of one race's cultural heritage. Wright (1970) also described cultural racism when he wrote:

> Until quite lately higher education in the United States of America has been almost completely under the sway of an illusion shared by nearly everybody of European descent since

> the Middle Ages—the illusion that the history
> of the world is the history of Europe and its
> cultural offshoots; that Western experience
> interpretations of that experience are sufficient,
> if not exhaustive; and that the resulting value
> systems embrace everything that matters.[110]

Clearly, this is an example of cultural racism. Cultural racism ignores the achievements of a race of people or interprets cultural differences negatively. It was not black Americans who were guilty of this behavior; instead, blacks responded to cultural racism by acknowledging and embracing their blackness and their unique contributions, which Du Bois eluded to in his use of the term *double consciousness.*

Pettigrew (1971) suggested that the charge of reverse racism may have resulted from a lack of understanding regarding the power base needed to enact racism as well as from the inability to perceive and accept black Americans as an ethnic group rather than just a racial group. What is amazing about the entire conversation surrounding the issue of race is that the pseudoscience about the biology of race had long been debunked. That this information had not reached the general public might not be surprising, but certainly for academics to behave as though black people constitute a racial rather than an ethnic group is surprising. In 1954 Allport, as stated earlier, explained how and why the appropriate name for human characteristics ascribed to race should be regarded as ethnic.

Allen's (1974) belief in the need to clarify the relationship of Black Studies to Ethnic Studies is an important one, for the two are often counterpoised and forced into antagonistic relationships. Race is based on physical criteria and ethnicity on cultural. Because cultural differences often accompany physical differences, there is a tendency to lump physical and cultural differences under the term *race*.[111] Black Studies differs from Ethnic Studies in that the former embraces both race or the misnomer of race and culture, whereas the latter may not.

When black students and faculty wanted programs staffed and run by blacks, they were not making new or even radical demands in higher education. Factors of ethnic background and experience had long played a role in hiring at colleges and universities in the United States.[112] An obvious example was in the hiring of teachers in foreign languages and literature. The people teaching Chinese language and literature were usually Chinese. Ethnic background had often been considered in other aspects of area studies and in other programs from the Peace Corps to social work. A number of scholars[113] suggested that the reluctance to grant that ethnic background should be considered when filling positions in Black Studies was reflective of cultural racism.

According to historian Winthrop Jordan (1969), cultural racism developed from ethnocentrism. Ethnocentrism, like prejudice, is an attitude. "Ethnocentrism becomes cultural racism when attitudes escalate into behaviors."[114] Ethnocentric attitudes cannot be transformed into cultural racism without the accumulation of power. Glenn (1965) described the kind of power that undergirded ethnocentric attitudes in the United States when he stated that whites were the majority of the population, constituted the majority of the college graduates, owned most of the wealth, occupied key social positions, as well as controlled the armed forces and the police force. They therefore had the power to prevent black economic and educational gains.[115] The ability to control, through the exercise of power, the lives and destinies of black Americans becomes cultural racism when those destinies are chained to white ethnocentric standards.[116] When black Americans must give up too extensive a portion of their own cultural heritage in order to enjoy the basic rights and privileges of American society, ethnocentrism has, according to Jones (1972), become cultural racism. The understanding of white power is crucial to the comprehension of black power. Jones correctly perceives that "[W]hen ethnocentric standards are used as a basis for national policy prescriptions, and buttressed by white power, the problems become increasingly acute. The issues of cultural racism are inextricably bound up with these cultural and power differentials,"[117] an argument used to refute the charges of racism in Black Studies.

Former Black Panther and law professor Kathleen Cleaver, in her article "The Antidemocratic Power of Whiteness,"[118] explains how white power is unrecognized by white Americans as she recalls Du Bois' comments on whiteness and its ability to disempower white workers, causing them to accept exploitation for the prize of being white. The very power of whiteness is an overwhelming factor that prevents Marxist and socialist theories of economics from taking root in the working-class and poor black communities throughout the United States.

The idea of cultural supremacy is by no means limited to Western culture, but according to Pettigrew (1971), no other culture has had the power to impose its cultural values and assumptions so widely. In higher education, cultural bias can be imposed through the use of standardized tests, IQ tests, and through the application of a variety of evaluation mechanisms that measure only Anglo-American norms and condemn deviations.[119] Cole and Gay (1971) found that difference in learning styles may be closely linked to culture. They conducted a study in the cross-cultural investigation of memory, comparing American and African students on their ability to memorize a list of twenty items. In test after test the Americans scored better than the Africans. Cole and Gay might have concluded that the Africans simply had an inferior memory. Instead they proceeded to use an element of African culture—they used the African oral tradition as the way of presenting the objects. They told a story in which each object was named. In this context, the African students learned every item on the list and recalled them in the exact order in which they had been named.[120] Other studies have compared differences in racial attitudes. In 1969 Campbell and Schuman reported the difference in white and black attitudes regarding the 1967 riots. White people thought the riots were planned in advance for the purpose of looting or for the general disruption of law and order. The riots were viewed as harmful to the cause of black Americans, and many felt the use of more police would prevent future riots.[121] Black Americans, in contrast, believed the riots were spontaneous reactions to racism and discrimination. They assumed the best way to avoid future riots was availability of more and better employment opportunities and an end to discrimination. These differences are described by Butler (1981) as differences in basic and cultural sensibilities.

The differences between ethnocentrism and racism may be one of attitude versus action as studies seem to indicate. Ethnocentrism is a judgment; it becomes racist when it escalates into behaviors, if one accepts Jones's definition of racism,[122] which states that racism is the transformation of race prejudice and/or ethnocentrism into powerful action against a group or individual that is identified as inferior. The exercise of power against the other can or cannot be intentional. The results are the same. Thus, it becomes apparent that ethnic studies—of which Black Studies is a part—in the context of American higher education is neither ethnocentric nor racist, but simply an attempt to redress past exclusionism. The stated goals, objectives, and philosophies of Black Studies, while diverse, have rarely, if ever, been to teach the racial superiority of black Americans.

Hare (1969), who coined the term *ethnic studies*, understood the intended purpose when he stated that Black Studies is based

> . . . ideally on the ideology of revolutionary nationalism. It is not based on any form of racism, black or white, though it is dedicated to the destruction of white racism. Which probably is why the establishment was determined—chiefly through its mass media—to confuse black students into a search for tangential, ultra separatist goals.[123]

While Hare advocated Black Studies programs that were autonomous, he insisted that "a black skin is no guarantee of a black mind: a white professor, if he has the same values and attitudes and orientation as a black professor, would make an excellent instructor for black studies courses."[124] He concluded that black racism may be theoretically true but practically speaking of little consequence.

In 1933 Du Bois, with reference to the scientific study of black Americans, was asked: "Is not this a program of segregation, emphasis on race, and particularism as against national unity and universal humanity?" His answer was simply, "It is, and it is not by choice but by force."[125] The force he referred to was racism. Anticipating the problem that would confront Black Studies, Du Bois also wrote:

> It is not ours to argue whether we will be segregated or whether we ought to be a caste. We are segregated: we are a caste. This is our given and at present unalterable fact. Our problem is how far and in what way can we consciously and scientifically guide our future so as to insure our physical survival, our spiritual freedom and our social growth?[126]

The struggle for Black Studies to find its place in higher education brought with it not only unwelcome charges and labels, but also the recognition of other ethnic groups as proper area studies. In 1977–78 Washburn (1981) reported that 3,038 institutions in the United States were surveyed, and of that number 439 provided 99,200 students with a total of 8,805 courses on 62 ethnic groups. There was a total of 316 majors offered, 283 minors, 58 graduate majors, 31 graduate minors, 240 bachelor degrees, 86 master's degrees, and 20 doctoral degrees.[127] Perhaps name calling has ceased, and a genuine effort toward cultural pluralism in American higher education has begun.

Today Black Studies celebrates its fortieth anniversary and is no longer the neophyte in the academy, as Women's Studies and/or Gender Studies and Queer studies have emerged as the newcomers. Black Studies opened the door for these and other area studies, just as the Civil Rights Movement encouraged other oppressed groups to demand their rights. Black Studies was the catalyst for diversity in higher education. Aldridge and Young (2000) outline the forty-year struggle and growth of Black Studies in the academy and discuss the growth and development of the field. Noliwe Rooks (2007) offers a provocative view of the growth of Black Studies based on white philanthropy.

W.E.B. Du Bois not only contributed the philosophical foundation for Black Studies as discussed in chapter 2, he also left a lasting, concrete contribution in the form of books and articles. What follows is a review of selected empirical and theoretical works relevant to the issues in Black Studies.

In 1897 Du Bois published "The Conservation of the Races" in *American Academy Occasional Papers, no. 2.* To conserve the races, which Du Bois had trouble defining because there is only one race, the human race, and he knew this, he stated what amounted to a Black Nationalist plea. He called for black colleges, newspapers, businesses, a "school of literature and art," that a later generation would name the black aesthetic. Self-help clearly was not only the domain of Garvey, Garveyism, or the Nation of Islam. Du Bois stated that "[O]ur one refuge is ourselves."[128] "The Conservation of the Races" is a seminal essay in the Du Bois canon, for it demonstrates his nationalist ideology and distinguishes his thought from the prevalent ideas espoused by Martin R. Delaney, Bishop Henry Mc Neil Turner, and others who concluded that the United States would never honor its ideal of democracy for black people. In Delaney's *The Condition, Elevation, Emigration and Destiny of the Colored People of the United States Politically Considered* (1852) he suggested that black people should establish a separate nation in South America or on the Caribbean islands. Du Bois, on the other hand, had not lost hope and suggested separation (not segregation) until such time as black people were recognized as full participants "in the kingdom of culture." He did not support emigration.

Some might argue that the time has now come when black people are full participants in the United States. Indeed some have said with the election of the first black president of the United States, we live in a "postracial society." Those who believe this to be true might question anew the need and purpose of Black Studies, historically black colleges and universities, and other nationalist survival methods. A warning from Du Bois echoes over the century: "Let us not deceive ourselves at our situation in this country."[129] Just how far have we advanced since this 1897 warning about the positionality of Black people in the United States? The answer is both negative and positive. Black people have made tremendous strides, and yet hatred toward Black people is not dead. Enough white people voted for President Obama in order for him to win the election, something that would not have occurred at the time Du Bois penned "Conservation." Nonetheless, threats against Barak Obama's life have since his election in 2008, quadrupled to greater than any number against any United States president— ever. MSNBC reported that the death threats were up 400 percent compared to those during the Bush administration.[130] We have come far, and still we have so far to go.

In 1898 "The Study of the Negro Problems" also appeared in *Annals of the American Academy of Political and Social Science*.[131] Du Bois in this essay argues for the intellectual validity of Black Studies, insisting that black people deserved "study for the great end of advancing the cause of science in general."[132] To fail to study the black experience in America would be to voluntarily support the ignorance that led to what he believed to be the causes of prejudice and racism, and would in fact support a hiatus in human knowledge. Du Bois also advocated the study of racism, calling it "Negro prejudice." He wanted the American Academy of Political and Social Science to isolate and study the tangible phenomena of prejudice in all of its aspects and outcomes. Studies should be made on the physical and mental development of black people affected by prejudice and racism. Du Bois believed that the results of living in a racist and oppressive system would lead to crime and lawlessness as well as affect the mental acquisitiveness of the people forced to live and function in such a system. He also knew that legal sanctions for crime were too often carried out based on prejudice.

The 1900 "Address to the Nations of the World," as he stood before the First Pan-African Conference, contains his most famous lines:

> The problem of the twentieth century is the problem of the color line, the question as to how far differences of race—which show themselves chiefly in the color of the skin and the texture of the hair—will hereafter be made the basis of denying to over half of the world the right of sharing to their utmost ability the opportunities and privileges of modern civilization.[133]

Du Bois would continue to attack the color line in speeches and essays throughout his long life. In "The Color Line Belts the World,"[134] he again repeats his pronouncement of the problem of the color line. He recognized that Americans want to be done with the problem, not by solving it, not by scientific study, and not by understanding it. They want to be relieved from even thinking about it. They are in fact tired of it. Du Bois warned that economic and political expansion brings white people into contact with people of the world who are in fact people of color, black and brown and what he called the yellow people of Asia. In this essay Du Bois said that although "the white races have had the hegemony of civilization . . . they have forgotten where civilization started."[135] They have led by "fear and force," which will not be eternal. He ends this short essay by asking if white behavior over people of color can be replaced by freedom and friendship.

Five years later, in 1911, Du Bois reported on the meeting of the First Universal Races Congress. The most important aspects of the congress, he pointed out, was that the majority of anthropologists had concluded that there is no "pure" race; that while differences in groups of people exist, it is not legitimate to argue that differences in physical characteristics are related to differences in mental characteristics; physical and mental characteristics are not permanent, and dispelling the Darwinian theory, as it was popularly conceived, this evolution did not take ages but could be modified with changes in education, environment and "public sentiment."[136] Given this river of knowledge, one of the anthropologists in attendance stated that people would continue to use race (this most unscientific term) to incite hatred instead of replacing it with a word that would imply brotherhood.

"The Training of Negroes for Social Power," appeared in *The Outlook,* October 17, 1903. In this piece Du Bois called for black Americans to assume responsibility for their own social regeneration. He stated that while black people must assume the responsibility, they must also be granted the power necessary to educate themselves and to control their lives through the acquisition of skills to enable them to earn a living. Social power would mean the growth of initiative among black people, the spread of independent thought; and these characteristics spread fear and distrust among whites at the same time that they demand social responsibility from blacks.

"The Talented Tenth" (1903), included in *The Negro Problem,* contains the wisdom that is sometimes glossed over when examining Du Bois' ideas as elitist. He said: "All men cannot go to college but some men must"[137;] and this was his rationale for the talented tenth. He believed that at least a tenth of the black population should be highly educated so that they could lift up the uneducated and undereducated masses. As stated previously, Du Bois was forced to abandon this idea and to look toward the masses to provide their own social uplift. In this same essay, Du Bois defines the university by stating that it is "a human invention for the transmission of knowledge and culture from generation to generation, through the training of quick minds and pure hearts, and for this work no other human invention will suffice, not even trade and industrial school."[138] By 1903 Du Bois had stated his clear opposition to Booker T. Washington, the greatest of the accommodationists regarding black higher education.

Du Bois' "Credo" appeared in *The Independent* (New York, October 6, 1904). Next to *The Souls of Black Folk,* this is his most well-known writing. In this brief two-page philosophical statement, Du Bois provided the rationale for much of what he endeavored to accomplish with regard to Black Studies. He stated unequivocally that he believed in black people and stated it in a language worth quoting:

> Especially do I believe in the Negro race; I believe in pride of race and lineage itself; in pride of self so deep as to scorn injustice to other selves; in pride of lineage so great as to despise no man's father; in pride of race so chivalrous as neither to offer bastardy to the weak nor beg wedlock of

the strong, knowing that men may be brothers
in Christ, even though they be no brothers-in-
law. . . . I believe in the Prince of Peace. I believe
that war is murder. I believe that armies and
navies are at bottom the tinsel and braggadocio
of oppression and wrong; and I believe that the
wicked conquest of weaker and darker nations
by nations white and stronger but foreshadows
the death of that strength.[139]

"We Claim Our Rights" was addressed to the Second
Annual Meeting of the Niagara Movement on August 16,
1906. (See *A Documentary History of the Negro People*,
Aptheker, 1951.) Here he gave a list of demands for Black
liberation. Regarding education he called for the United
States government to step up and wipe out illiteracy and to
support education that would develop "power and ideal."
This essay was followed by "The Value of Agitation," which
appeared in *The Voice of the Negro* (Atlanta), v. 14, (March
1907). A reporter had accused Du Bois of being an agitator because of the militant tone of his many statements.
Du Bois responded as follows: "The man that has a griev-
ance is supposed to speak for himself. No one can speak
for him[;] no one knows the thing as well as he does. It is
then high time that the Negro agitator should be in the
land."[140] Du Bois, forced by the circumstances of the place
and time in which he lived, assumed the role of agitator,
activist, and even politician; none of which he had ever
planned to do.

"The Evolution of the Race Problem," a paper delivered
at the National Negro Conference on June 1, 1909, and published in *Proceedings of the National Negro Conference*,[141]
challenged the scientific racism of the day, which claimed
to show that Black people were genetically inferior. Du

Bois wrote: "I for one have protested and do protest and shall protest that in my humble opinion the assumption of racial inferiority is an outrageous falsehood dictated by selfishness, cowardice and greed and for the righteousness of my cause and the proof of my assertions, I appeal to one arbitrament and one alone and that is: the truth."[142]

Here also Du Bois raises research questions that can be answered through Black Studies. He asked, What is the truth? What is the truth regarding Black life in America and in the world? Has Black Studies made the kind of systematic effort on a scale that Du Bois suggested to ascertain the facts regarding Black crime, poverty, and education? In 1909, he claimed that "not a single systematic effort to answer these questions on an adequate scale [had] been made in these United States from 1619 to 1909."[143] The reluctance to provide adequate funding and support for the kind and breadth of program that Du Bois conceived still plagues Black Studies today.

The address "Race Prejudice," was presented on March 5, 1910, at the Republican Club of New York City. Du Bois' prophesy in this speech reminds one of the Reverend Jeremiah Wright, President Barack Obama's former pastor. He declared that "America is not liked in the darker world" because it has gone out of its way to "insult many of these people. [It] has enslaved 'niggers,' sneered at 'dagos,' insulted Chinese and Japanese, and found no words too contemptuous to express . . . feeling for the 'mongrel' races of Central and Southern America."[144] These audacious comments regarding the United States' relationship with the third world and the economic price the United States will have to pay because of its racism grabbed attention and criticism; but again, Du Bois correctly predicted attitudes and situations he did not live to see, one example being the American hostage situation in Iran and more recently the September 11, 2001, terror attack.

Speaking before the Senate Committee on February 2, 1912, Du Bois presented "How to celebrate the Semicentennial of the Emancipation Proclamation."[145] He proposed a panoramic exhibition of black culture from Egyptian civilization to current events. He wanted the exhibit to be a permanent collection housed in a museum, and reminded the Senate Committee that there was an African Exhibit in London and in Paris but nothing of the sort in the United States. In 1913 Du Bois presented his pageant of the black race, "The Star of Ethiopia," in New York City. The exhibition appeared with the support of the NAACP. According to Foner "thirty thousand people visited the exposition."[146] This pageant represented an early example of Du Bois' theory of black art.

"The African Roots of War" appeared in *The Atlantic Monthly*.[147] An important essay that presents an alternative view of the cause of World War I, Du Bois emphasized the role that European imperialism played on the continent of Africa and how colonialism was responsible for the war. He also traced the roots of racism and color prejudice. Du Bois believed that color was not always linked with prejudice and racism, but became linked when "the world began to invest in color prejudice. The 'color line' began to pay dividends."[148] Du Bois is not alone in his belief about the origin of racism and its economic roots. Africa was not always another name for bestiality and barbarism. Indeed, Timbuktu was the center of learning to which whites traveled, as were Alexandra and other African sites. One can but wonder whether pure economics can be the cause for the venomous hatred expressed in color prejudice and racism. Perhaps a commingling of both economic and psychological issues that racists suffer from are to blame.[149]

"The Future of Africa: A Platform" was read at a mass meeting sponsored by the NAACP on January 6, 1919, at Carnegie Hall in New York City. Du Bois used irony to make his points, but sadly his points seem more true than ironic. He said that people know that Africa is not a continent without a history or civilization, and yet the *Encyclopedia Britannica* referred to Africa as a continent without a history, and that the rise of black people in Africa, the West Indies, and the United States is easy enough to see. To refuse to see the truth, he said, is "nothing more than a vicious habit of mind."[150] A habit, he claimed, that can be lost as easily as belief in war, sexism against women, fear of education for the masses, and our belief in the necessity of poverty.[151] However, for the most part, these habits have not been easily overcome.

In the Red Summer of 1919, Du Bois was outraged by the treatment of returning black servicemen who had fought for the United States in good faith and at his urging. As editor of *The Crisis*, Du Bois had encouraged blacks to support the war effort because he believed the idea of fighting to make the world safe for democracy would cause white Americans to recognize their own hypocrisy, on one hand, saving the world, while on the other hand, supporting their own racist and undemocratic policies at home. Du Bois miscalculated, and the soldiers returned to the same segregation and Jim Crow laws they had left.

In *Darkwater* (1920) one essay in particular stands out: "The Souls of White Folk" further developed Du Bois' concept of "double consciousness" that he introduced in *The Souls of Black Folk* (1903). This essay explains the unusual vantage point of black Americans, a position that allows blacks to view whites as perhaps no one else can. Du Bois says this second sight is more than the knowledge a servant has for a master, more than what the masses perceive of certain classes. The reason he gives for this deep knowing is that black people are "native, not foreign, bone of their thought and flesh of their language."[152] The closeness allows blacks to see whites undressed and from the backside. Du Bois claims black people know the workings of their entrails, know their thoughts, and this intimate knowledge embarrasses them and causes them to deny the rights of blacks. Du Bois ends the passage by writing, "They deny my right to live and be and call me misbirth! My word is to them mere bitterness and my soul, pessimism. And yet as they preach and strut and shout and threaten, crouching as they clutch at rags of facts and fancies to hide their nakedness, they go twisting, flying by. . . . I see them ever stripped—ugly, human."[153] In *Darkwater,* poetry mixes with prose, irony with sarcasm, comprising the elements that characterize Du Bois' essays.

While Du Bois was a promoter of race pride for minorities, he also was aware of the problems this promotion was likely to represent to the larger society. The "race pride" movement of the 1920s raised some of the same issues as the "Black Is Beautiful" movement of the 1960s. On the issue of race pride Du Bois wrote the following in *The Crisis.*[154]

> Today Negroes, Indians, Chinese, and other groups, are gaining new faith in themselves; they are discovering that the current theories and stories of "backward" peoples are largely lies and assumptions; that human genius and possibility are not limited by color, race, or blood. What is this new self-consciousness leading to?

> Inevitably and directly to distrust and hatred of
> whites; to demands for self-government, sepa-
> ration, driving out of foreigners; "Asia for Asi-
> atics," "Africa for Africans," and "Negro officers
> for Negro troops!" No sooner do whites see this
> unawaited development than they point out in
> dismay the inevitable consequences: "you lose
> our tutelage," "you spurn our knowledge," "you
> need our wealth and technique."

Du Bois' words are as accurate in 2009 as they were in 1920. He argued that whites must choose one or the other: They must either "leave people of color alone, withdraw from foreign lands, give black Americans our states and towns and sections and let black people rule themselves. . . . Absolutely segregate the races of the world," he declared, "or meet the people of the world as equals."[155] Clearly, Du Bois preferred the latter but could if necessary live with the former. While his first proposition resonates with the concepts articulated by Elijah Muhammad and Malcolm X in the Nation of Islam (NOI), it predates the NOI. Unlike Garvey and the black leaders who called for emigration to Africa or to other parts of the world, Du Bois insisted that black labor, black blood, sweat, and tears had purchased our place in the United States.

The other salient point of this essay relative to Black Studies is the position that whites should hold in the programs and departments. Du Bois in "Race Pride," stated it should be "possible for whites to rise to the highest position in China and Uganda and blacks to the highest honors in England and Texas. Here is the choice. Which will you have, my masters?"[156] At such time when things are equal, then the question might cease to exist.

In Black Studies the knowledge base appropriate for curriculum development was another issue of contention. Du Bois defined knowledge by stating what it was not. In his 1930 commencement address at Howard University,[157] Du Bois stated his "Ideal of Knowledge." He said it was not guess work, not mere careless theory; not inherited religious dogma clung to because of fear and inertia and in spite of logic, but critically tested and laboriously gathered fact marshaled under scientific law and feeding rather than choking the glorious world of fancy and imagination, of poetry and art, of beauty and deep culture.[158] Of Black Studies, Turner echoes Du Bois, stating that "A social science bereft of an analysis of the interchange between the subjective and the objective is thus a social science orientation that condones a tendency of 'uncritical acceptance of ideological bias.'"[159]

"The Field and Function of the American Negro College" first appeared in *Fisk News*, v. 6, no. 10 (June 1933) and is an address to the General Alumni Association, Fisk University. Here Du Bois commented on the necessity of relevance in education to real life experiences and warns again against cultural chauvinism, a warning often directed to the student activists during their push for Black Studies in the academy. Du Bois wrote:

> A university is made of human beings, learning of the things they do not know from things they do know in their own lives . . . human culture in its broadest and finest sense can never be wholly the product of the few. There is no natural aristocracy of man, either within a nation or among the races of the world, which unless fed copiously from without can build up and maintain and diversify a broad human

culture. A system of national education which tries to confine its benefits to preparing the few for the life of the few, dies of starvation. (N.p.)

In this address Du Bois also set forth an expanded definition of race, that problematic term we still face. Moving from his sociohistorical definition offered in the "Conservation of the Races" essay, he insisted that it is beside the point to ask whether black people form a real race, and said, "Biologically we are mingled of all conceivable elements, but race is psychology, not biology; and psychologically we are a unified race with one history, one red memory and one revolt" (n.p.).

Undoubtedly, today the idea of "one red memory" would be challenged. Philosopher Tommy Lott points out that Du Bois has been critiqued for not acknowledging the differences among the historical experiences of various black groups, stating that Du Bois' "sociohistorical notion seems to break down when applied to culturally distinct groups of black people."[160] Du Bois' idea of a unified race is essentialist with the essential element being the oppression of black people. Anthony Appiah has pointed out that oppression is not unique to black people.[161] However, Lott correctly suggests that Du Bois' use of the oppression of black people is essentialist in the same way that anti-Semitism is an essential force that binds together Jews.[162]

In the commentary "On Segregation"[163] Du Bois responded to the charge that in the fight for integration black people were trying to escape themselves. He writes: One must fight with his brains, and above all, know what one is fighting for. One is fighting to say to the world: The opportunity of knowing Negroes is worth so much to us and is so appreciated, that we want you to know them too. The 1934 *Crisis* article was not the first time that Du Bois had to respond to the charge of self-hatred. A year earlier, in a 1933 article, "On Being Ashamed of Oneself" (*The Crisis*), Du Bois admitted that black people were indeed ashamed of themselves. He explained that in working hard to become assimilated into white American culture and society, the successful, educated black person is loath to be identified with the so-called common element. This essay appears to contradict the previous one; however, both statements regarding black pride are true. Those Black people who were working for integration were doing so because they were proud of themselves. At the same time they were also ashamed, but not of themselves. Rather, they were ashamed and afraid of being lumped together with the lower classes of uneducated, "ill-mannered," and even criminal elements. The problem of class is an issue to be dealt with by "a new organized group action along economic lines,"[164] according to Du Bois.

In a 1911 article "Ashamed" (*The Crisis*) the issue behind the charges from whites that black people were ashamed of their race when they were dissatisfied with the treatment they received, Du Bois exposed what he called the curious logic in their syllogism. "White men alone are men. This Negro wants to be a man. Ergo, he wants to be a white man."[165] Again Du Bois' answer was that those who are ashamed submit and do not fight for freedom. While he encouraged race pride, Du Bois also cautioned black people against hubris. The crucial element in his advice for Black Studies was the warning not to become entrapped in exaggerated claims such as, "the black race is the first and greatest of races, that its accomplishments are most extraordinary, that its desert is most obvious and mistakes negligible."[166] Du Bois knew the rhetoric of a people either white or black with a superiority complex. He said that on the part of black people such talk cannot be avoided because it is just as true and just as false as it is with all races. The examples in the Black Studies Movement were clear. Many programs started with the hagiography of African kings and queens. On the other hand, the study of Western civilization also began with the study of kings and queens.

"Does the Negro Need Separate Schools?"[167] is an important essay because it challenges black people to recognize their own power. It focuses on Black Power in terms of belief and self-confidence. The essay begins Du Bois' most clear articulation of black nationalism. He said, "twelve million American Negroes have the inborn capacity to accomplish just as much as any nation of twelve million anywhere in the world ever accomplished, and this is not because they are Negroes but because they are human."[168] The "Separate Schools" essay states clearly that black people constitute a nation within a nation; and he chastises blacks for not having more confidence in their own institutions. He argued that as long as "Negroes believe that their race is constitutionally and permanently inferior to white people, they necessarily disbelieve in every possible Negro institution."[169] This statement probably was the most disconcerting that Du Bois would make, one that angered the NAACP and middle-class leaders who were working for integration at all costs. Du Bois was not against integration in terms of public access. Rather, he was against putting black children at risk and believed they would not learn in hostile environments.

Even more clearly articulated in the essay "A Negro Nation Within the Nation"[170] is the elaboration of Du Bois' statement regarding black nationalism. He argued that for all intents and purposes a black nation does exist. Further, he declared that it had "been partially accomplished in the organization of the Negro retail business; the great majority of American Negroes are divided not only for religious but for a large number of social purposes into self-supporting economic units, self-government, self-directed."[171] While this essay is nationalist in its sentiments, Du Bois was not, as some have argued,[172] a Black Nationalist in the sense that he had no desire for integration. In fact, he argued both for separation—not segregation—black economic power and for integration when it could be achieved on the basis of complete equality.

In 1936 Du Bois wrote an essay, "Negro and the New Deal," that catalogues the experiences of black people from 1933 to 1936, during the heart of the Depression. Within the study he included the "Basic American Negro Creed," which he summarized, using the correspondence of other black scholars. This creed included four statements as a preamble and eleven points, the first two of which are listed below and state a clear philosophy regarding black life in the United States.[173]

> As American Negroes, we believe in the unity of racial effort, so far as this is necessary for self-defense and self-expression, leading ultimately to the goal of a united humanity and the abolition of all racial distinctions. We repudiate all artificial and hate-engendering deification of race separation as such; but just as sternly, we repudiate an enervating philosophy of Negro escape into an artificially privileged white race which has long sought to enslave, exploit and tyrannize over all mankind.

This first statement clarifies Du Bois' nationalist position and sets it apart from the NOI and other late twentieth-century groups.

A major aspect of *Dusk of Dawn* (1940) is contained in its subtitle: *An Essay Toward an Autobiography of a Race Concept.* The idea and concept of race continued to preoccupy Du Bois. In chapter 5 of the book, "The Concept of Race," he questioned the relationship between himself and Africa. The relationship is a feeling that he found difficult to explain. He settled on the idea of a common historical experience, a "common disaster"—which today is referred to as the African Maafa (the middle passage and slavery)—and "one long memory" (1940). Pan-Africanism was an important aspect of Du Bois' concept of Black Studies. Du Bois stated in "The Concept of Race" that it was in Africa that he began to clearly comprehend the connection between race and wealth. The kinship with Africa and with what he called "the children of Africa" finds expression in Africana Studies.

In 1949 "The Freedom to Learn"[174] article addressed intellectual freedom. Du Bois wrote that freedom is always dangerous and is never complete. But given these circumstances, "the freedom to learn . . . is the least dangerous."[175] In another important essay regarding freedom, "The Nature of Intellectual Freedom," he states that if ignorance is ever to be conquered, people must be forced to learn. A taxing question that confronts professors of Black Studies and curriculum designers is: To what extent should courses in Black Studies be required? It still is possible to graduate from a college or university in the United States without knowing black history or culture, and yet the presence of recalcitrant learners or those who intentionally aim to disrupt the learning process has discouraged many educators from including Black Studies as part of the educational core requirements.

"The Future and Function of the Private Negro College"[176] (1960) is an essay in which Du Bois defined cultural heritage as "a careful Knowledge of the Past out of which the group as such has emerged."[177] This knowledge must include African history and the history of our development in the United States, Canada, Mexico, the Caribbean, South America, and throughout the entire Diaspora. Then Du Bois declares that it is not enough to know just about ourselves and our experience in the "New World" or the experiences through which our ancestors have come. We need to understand ourselves and the world. Whether or not we recognize it, the ancestral experience is "part of our bone and sinew," he said. We need to understand the differences and similarities of the social problems of the Caribbean, South and Central America, not only among black people but those affecting Native Americans and other minority groups. Du Bois insisted the future of black life depended on how well the lessons of the past instructed and influenced our dreams and plans. The plans for black life "cannot stem from empty air or successfully be based on the experiences of others alone." He asked, "Shall we seek to ignore our background and graft ourselves on a culture which does not wholly admit us, or build anew on that marvelous African art heritage . . . [?] Whence shall our drama come, from ourselves today or from Shakespeare in the English seventeenth century?"[178] Of integrationists Du Bois said that they might not realize what they were giving up. "In their haste to become American, their desire not to be peculiar or segregated in mind or body, they try to escape their cultural heritage and the body of experiences which they themselves have built up."[179] An appreciation of black history and culture would make clear the need to conserve the black cultural heritage that Du Bois described.

With civil rights and social equality becoming more of a reality for black Americans, Du Bois, in "Whither Now and Why," from *The Education of Black People: Ten Critiques 1906–1960,*[180] like James Baldwin[181] who advised against integrating into the burning house of the United States, warned that integration was not a panacea for the problems facing Black people. He said:

> [I]t brings not as many assume an end to the so-called Negro problem, but a beginning of even more difficult problems of race and culture. . . . Are we to assume that we will simply adopt the ideals of Americans and become what they are or want to be and that we will have in this process no ideals of our own? That would mean that we would cease to be Negroes as such and become white in action if not completely in color.[182]

Du Bois says complete assimilation would solve the racial problem with black people committing racial suicide. In this writing Du Bois also addresses the charge of black racism with these words:

> Any statement of our desire to develop Negro culture, to keep up our ties with colored people, to remember our past is being regarded as "racism" [but] what I have been fighting for and am still fighting for is the possibility of black folk and their cultural patterns existing in America without discrimination; and on terms of equality. If we take this attitude we have got to do so

consciously and deliberately. . . . What we must also do is to lay down a line of action which will accomplish two things: the utter disappearance of color discrimination in American life and the preservation of African history and culture as a valuable contribution to modern civilization as it was to medieval and ancient civilization.[183]

The foregoing quotations touch upon nearly every issue raised with regard to Black Studies programs in American higher education. Du Bois' philosophical statements reveal that his contributions on one level have been critical and prophetic. On another level his works show that the same issues and problems exist today as when Du Bois first attacked them. Du Bois' analysis of black American intellectual freedom and the issue now being hotly debated over the future and function of the black college is an example of the breadth of his vision.

Annotated Bibliography: Du Bois' Contributions to the Subject Matter of Black Studies

All of the following works were either written or edited by Du Bois. They are arranged according to the various disciplines or subject areas in Black Studies.

History

1892 "The enforcement of the Slave-Trade laws," *Annual Report of the American Historical Association for the Year 1891.* Senate Document 173, 52nd Congress, 1st session, Washington, DC. Presents some of the research Du Bois must have conducted for his dissertation.

1896 *The Suppression of the African Slave Trade to the United States 1638–1870*, New York: Longmans, Green. 335pp. Treats slavery in the colonies, and the American Revolution; and analyzes the impact of the Haitian Revolution on the suppression of slavery.

1901 "The Freedmen's Bureau," *Atlantic Monthly* 87 (March): 354–65. An historical analysis of the bureau.

1901 "The Negro Landholder of Georgia," *Bulletin of the Department of Labor* 6 (July):647–777.

1905 "The Niagara Movement," *Voice of the Negro* 2 (Sept.):619–22. Traces Du Bois' s role in the development of this movement.

1909 *John Brown*. Philadelphia: George Jacobs. 406pp. An extensive biography that treats John Brown from a black perspective.

1915 *The Negro*. New York: Henry Holt. 254pp. Contains a history of Africa, and traces black development in the United States, the Caribbean, and Central America. Indicates Du Bois' growing interest in Africa and the Diaspora but is marked by some of the prevailing prejudices of the sources from which Du Bois obtained his information.

1924 *The Gift of Black Folk: Negroes in the Making of America*. 190 pp. Boston: Stratford. This book traces the contributions of Black Americans to the United States from pre-Columbian times to the 1920s. It is well documented containing 179 footnotes.

1930 *Africa: Its Geography, People and Products.* 63 pp. Kansas: Haldeman-Julius. Describes African geography and compares it to European. Also describes African languages and religions.

1930 *Africa; Its Place in History*. 63 pp. Kansas: Haldeman-Julius. Concentrates on modern African history, outlines African resistance to colonialism and imperialism.

1935 *Black Reconstruction in America, 1860–1880*. 746 pp. New York: Harcourt, Brace. Exposes the propaganda of history; uses quotations from current textbooks to illustrate his points. Extensive references. 1992 edition edited by David Levering Lewis. New York: Atheneum. This is a classic.

1939 *Black Folk, Then and Now: An Essay in the History and Sociology of the Negro Race.* 401 pp. New York; Henry Holt. Contains 16 chapters and an exhaustive bibliography. Begins with ancient African history and civilization and ends with a documentation of third world uprisings against oppression.

1945 *Color and Democracy: Colonies and Peace.* 143 pp. New York: Harcourt, Brace. States that "colonies are the slums of the world." Points out that the majority of the worlds' people are people of color.

1948 "Race Relations in the United States, 1917–1947." *Phylon* 9:234–47. A progress report, that race relations had improved because of changed attitudes, growth in the black population, and a concerted effort on the part of black people to sue for their rights.

1947 *The World and Africa: An Inquiry into the Part Which Africa has Played in World History,* 276 pp. New York: Viking. Begins with the decline and fall of Europe. Examines the slave trade, traces a variety of cultural and racial groups in Africa, and ends with a discussion of Africa's modern nations.

Sociology

1897 The Atlanta University studies, 1897–1910. Edited by Du Bois. Contains over a thousand pages of sociological and anthropological information on black Americans.

1898 "The Study of Negro Problems," *Annals of the American Academy of Political and Social Science* 219, no. 11, 1–23. Defines what the so-called Negro problems are, and outlines what must be done to solve them.

1899 *The Philadelphia Negro.* 520 pp. Philadelphia: University of Pennsylvania. A social study of the black population in the city of Philadelphia. A classic. Reprinted 1973. Introduction by Aptheker. New York: Kraus-Thomson.

1903 "The Laboratory in Sociology at Atlanta," *Annals of the American Academy of Political Science* 21 (May):160–63. A good review of the research methodology Du Bois used during his early tenure at Atlanta University.

1932 "Black Folk and Birth Control." *Birth Control Review* 16 (June): 166–67. Du Bois approved the idea of birth control and did not consider it a plan for black genocide as did some nationalist leaders of the 1960s.

POLITICAL SCIENCE

1920 "The Republicans and the Black Voter." *The Nation* 110 (June 5):757–58. Demonstrates that in several states black voters had the power to determine winners.

1933 "The South and a Third Party." *New Republic* 33 (January 3): 138–41. Argues that a third party system is almost impossible due to the disfranchisement of blacks in the South.

1940 "As the Crow Flies." Column in *The Amsterdam News* (June 1). Discusses the politics of Pan-Africanism using the life of Malaku Bayen, Haile Selassie's personal physician. Bayen had attended Howard University Medical School and married a black American woman, Dorothy Hadley.

1945 "The Winds of Time." Column in *The Chicago Defender*, (June 9). Speaks out against racism in California. Says that racism restricts not only blacks but Jews, Asians and Mexican-Americans.

1945 "The Winds of Time." *The Chicago Defender*. (June 2). Criticizes the University of California at Berkeley for conferring an honorary degree upon Jan Smuts of South Africa's Apartheid regime.

1947 "The Most Hopeful State in the World." *Soviet Russia Today*, 16 (November):24. Praises the accomplishments of the U.S.S.R.

1948 "From McKinley to Wallace: My Fifty Years as a Political Independent." *Masses and Mainstream* 1(August):3–13.

Defends Henry Wallace and the Progressive Party. Du Bois voted for Wallace.

1956 "Colonialism and the Russian Revolution." *New World Review* (November), 24: 18–22. Looked favorably on the Russian Revolution.

1958 "The Negro and Socialism." *Towards a Socialist America.* H. Alfred, ed. New York: Peace, pp. 278–91. Says Blacks should study socialism to see how it can be applied to their situation.

1959 "China and Africa." *New World Review.* 24 (November):18–22. Urges Africans to study socialism and reject capitalist materialism.

Autobiography

1920 *Darkwater: Voices from within the Veil.* New York: Harcourt, Brace. 276 pp. A collection of essays, family history, and other autobiographical facts. Contains Du Bois' "Credo", "A Litany at Atlanta" and the essays "The Souls of White Folk" and "The Damnation of Women."

1940 *Dusk of Dawn: An Essay Toward an Autobiography of a Race Concept.* New York: Harcourt, Brace. 334 pp. A more extensive statement of his intellectual life but focused on race and his effort to define it.

1968 *The Autobiography of W.E.B. Du Bois.* New York: International Publishers. 448 pp. A complete autobiography published posthumously and edited by Herbert Aptheker.

Essays

1903 *The Souls of Black Folk: Essays and Sketches.* Chicago: A.C. McClung. 264pp. Contains essays on slavery, emancipation, black music, and the now famous criticism on Booker T. Washington's educational and political views.

1901 "The Relation of the Negroes to the Whites in the South." *Annals of the American Academy of Political and Social Science* 18 (July): 121–140. Says that the "survival of the fittest shall mean the triumph of the good. Race relations will improve with conscientious study.

1901 "The Black North." *New York Times Magazine Supplement.* (November 17, 24, December 1, 8, 15). A series of five articles: two on New York City, one on Philadelphia and Boston, and one entitled, "Some Conclusions." All expose Northern racism.

1906 "The Color Line Belts the World." *Collier's.* 28 (October): 30. Japan's defeat of czarist Russia in 1905 marked the beginning of the end of white supremacy, according to Du Bois.

1924 "The Negro Takes Stock." *New Republic.* 37 (January):143–145. Warns of violence if Jim Crow is continued.

1928 "The Name Negro." *The Crisis.* 35 (March):96-97. Said the name Negro was as good as any other.

1931 "Will the Church Remove the Color Line?" *Christian Century*, 48 (December 9):1554–56. His answer is no. Reviews the role of major churches in the fight for human rights and finds them wanting.

1947 "Can the Negro Expect Freedom by 1965?" *Negro Digest* 5 (April): 4–9. His answer is yes, but he questions black values. He asks if black people will use education for enjoyment or for service.

NOVELS

1911 *The Quest for the Silver Fleece.* Chicago: A.C. McClury. 434 pp. Reprinted 1969. Miami: Mnemosyne. Love story that also articulates the problems of racism.

1928 *Dark Princess: A Romance.* New York: Harcourt, Brace. 311p. The story of a worldwide conspiracy of third world people to overthrow white imperialism. The movement is led by an Indian princess (not a Native American).

1959–61 *The Black Flame.* Trilogy. Tells what life was like for black people in the United States from 1876 to 1956. Uses actual historical figures and authentic quotations.

Drama

1908 "The Christ of the Andes." *Horizon*.4 (November-December): 1–14. Two scenes appear in the *Horizon*. A protest drama against war.

1911 "The Star of Ethiopia." A drama Du Bois wrote and produced for a national emancipation celebration. The play is a dance drama and pageant that presents the history of black people in Africa and in America. First produced in New York City, then in Philadelphia, in Washington, D.C., and finally it was produced at the Hollywood Bowl. The play was seen by more than 100,000 people. (W. Wilson, ed. 1970 *Black Folk: A Pageant for the Centenary, 1732–1932*. New York: New American Library).

Poetry

1899 "The Song of the Smoke." *Horizon*. 7 (January) 132. The famous lines from this poem are: "I will be black and blackness can/the blacker the mantle the mightier the man."

1906 "A Litany at Atlanta." *Independent* 61 (October): 856–58. Du Bois' most famous poem. Written after the Atlanta race massacre.

1907 "My Country' Tis of Thee." *Horizon* (November): 7. A parody that mocks democracy for Blacks in the United States. Begins: My country tis of thee/late land of slavery.

1914 "A Christmas Poem." *Crisis*. (December). A powerful poem that features the persona (presumably white) in conversation with God trying to explain the rape of Africa, war, and the lynching of American Blacks.

1914 "The Burden of Black Women." *Crisis*. (November). A dramatic poem. The following is a characteristic line: "Black mother of the iron hills that guard the blazing sea,/Wild spirit of a storm-swept soul a-struggling to be free."

1926 "The Song of America." *Herald Tribune*. (October): 18. Sardonic critique of false democracy.

1953 "The Rosenbergs." *Masses & Mainstreams*. 6 (July): 10–12. Emotional poems on what Du Bois saw as a miscarriage of justice.

1964 *Selected Poems*. Accra: Ghana University Press.42 pp. Never distributed.

SHORT STORY

1887 "Tom Brown at Fisk." *Fisk Herald* 5 (December, January 1888, and March 1888): 5–7; 6–7. Story of Tom and Ella and how education makes leaders for the good of the black masses.

1903 "Of the Coming of John." In *The Souls of Black Folk*. Poignantly describes the crisis of the black intellectual.

1907 "Wittekind." (note: name of Saxon leader who opposed the French in Saxon War.) In the short story it is the name of the ship bringing whites to the United States. *Horizon* 1 (April): 9–10. Today the story would be called flash fiction. Contains only 23 lines. The main point concerns the exploding population of blacks in South Carolina.

1907 "The Case." *Horizon* 2. (July): 4–10. Story narrated by a train porter about a mysterious woman and a train wreck.

1911 "Jesus Christ in Georgia." In *Crisis*, (December) A surrealistic story of Christ observing racism in Georgia.

1918 "Steve." *Crisis*. 17 (December): 62–63. About a dog, possibly autobiographical about his wife and daughter and the death of their pet.

1919 "The Gospel according to Mary Brown." *Crisis*. 19 (December): 41–43. Black interpretation of Mary, the mother of Jesus. The key question Du Bois poses is: "Would his Father send a black boy to this world just to make him suffer?

1923 "On Being Crazy." *Crisis*. 26 (June): 56–57. Humorous story about social equality between blacks and whites.

1933 "The Son of God." *Crisis*. 40 (December): 276–277. Another black interpretation of the immaculate conception, except in Du Bois' story Joe smacks Mary in the face!

CRITICISM

1913 "The Negro in Literature and Art." *Annals of the American Academy of Political and Social Science.* 49 (September):233–37. Concludes that Black Americans are artistic and says their talent should not be disparaged.

1916 "The Drama Among Black Folk." *Crisis.* 22:169–73. Traces the history of black people in the dramatic arts.

1923 "Can the Negro Save the Drama?" *Theatre Magazine.* 38 (July):12,68. Says that the black experience provides rich material for use in drama.

1927 "The Krigwa Players Little Negro Theatre." *Amsterdam News.* (October). The Krigwa Players was a Black American theatre Company Du Bois started in 1925. The company disbanded in 1927. This article summarizes two years of the group' s activities.

1926 "Criteria of Negro Art." *Crisis.* 32(October):290–97. Discusses how art is used as propaganda. Says that black people have the same right to use propaganda in art as others. He declared: "I don't give a damn for art that is not propaganda."

1929 "Freedom in Art Must be Fought For." *Journal and Guide.* (July 30). Formulates ideas on the black aesthetic. Says that back artist must create for black audiences, not white ones.

1931 "Beside the Still Waters." *Crisis,* 38 (May):168–69. Examines the relationship between blacks and the American theater.

1941 "The Vision of Phillis the Blessed. An Allegory of Negro American Literature in the Eighteenth and Nineteenth Centuries." A brief review of black writers prior to the twentieth century.

ECONOMICS

1906 "The Economic Future of the Negro." *Publications of the American Economic Association.* 7 (February): 219–242.

Perhaps the earliest study of the economy of black Americans. Emphasizes class differences among blacks.

1907 "The Economic Revolution in the South." In *The Negro in the South*, Philadelphia: G.W. Jacobs. A lecture given at the Philadelphia Divinity School. Du Bois said that the South lagged behind the rest of the industrial nation because of slavery and the system of sharecropping that followed.

1910 "The Economic Aspects of Race Prejudice." *Editorial Review*, 2(May): 488–493. Points out the capitalistic motives behind dividing workers.

1911 "The Economics of Negro Emancipation in the United States." *Sociological Review.* 4 (October):303–313. Concludes that emancipation must be economic, not political.

1924 "To the American Federation of Labor." *Crisis*, 28 (August):153–54. Attacks their racist policies.

1930 "Economic Disfranchisement." *Crisis* 37(August):281–82. Discusses the need for public ownership of public services.

1930 "Employment." *Crisis* 37 (October):353–54. Warns against blaming the victim for unemployment.

1931 "The Negro's Industrial Plight." *Crisis* 38 (July):241–42. Concerned with black unemployment. Recommends Herman Feldman's *Racial Factors in American Industry* (1931) as necessary reading to understand the situation of black unemployment.

1950 "Negroes and the Crisis of Capitalism in the United States." *Monthly Review* 4 (April):178–85. Du Bois warns against the glitter of industrialism and the selfishness of conspicuous consumption.

REFERENCE

1903 *A Bibliography of Negro Folk Songs.* Atlanta: Atlanta University Press, 8 pp.

1939 "The Negro Scientist." *American Scholar* 8 (Summer):309–320. Describes the contributions of Black American chemists, physicians, biologists, and others. Concludes that scientific progress is inhibited by racism.

1945 *Encyclopedia of the Negro: Preparatory Volume with References Lists and Reports.* New York: Phelps-Stokes Fund, 208pp.

The foregoing is but a partial listing of Du Bois' concrete contributions to the subject matter of Black Studies. Du Bois contributed regularly to newspapers and wrote countless book reviews that comprise valuable criticism on black American art and literature. He also commented on literature written by and/or about blacks in general. Du Bois also wrote for children. In 1920 he founded and edited the *Brownies' Book*, a monthly magazine for black children. Du Bois' writing challenged the authority of his day. Scholars of his day either attacked or "studiously ignored" black history and culture. Therefore, Du Bois constantly moved against the tide of current popular research. In so doing, his works, which contain the theoretical basis for Black Studies, have been suppressed and fragmented. This study has been an effort to synthesize his works as they relate to Black Studies.

CHAPTER 5

HIS DEEP AND ABIDING LOVE

I am resolved to defend the poor and the weak
of every race and hue, and especially to guard
my mother, my wife, my daughter and all my
darker sisters from the insults and aggressions
of white men and black, with the last strength of
my body and the last suffering of my soul.

—"I am Resolved" 1912

In addition to advocating for the study of the black
experience in the United States, Du Bois was an early
advocate for women's rights. His contributions to black
Women's Studies are among the first, along with Frederick
Douglass, to establish the legacy of black men advocating
for gender justice. Even though his biographer (Lewis) has
pointed out that regarding his relationship with women
he could talk the talk better than he could actually walk
the walk, his philosophical position was more correct than
most men of his day and class.[1] He was among the earliest

men to recognize the importance of women's contribution to family income. In "The Damnation of Women"[2] he said the freedom for women was next to the color line. Had he been a woman he might have said that it is part and parcel of the color line. That is, women experience color and sexual discrimination simultaneously. Historian Joy James believes that Du Bois did not use the words "next to" to indicate "sequential order of descending importance," [3] but that he understood the issue of women's freedom as a complicating factor in the color line. What he intended at the time he wrote the essay we will never know, but his actions and other writings confirm that in rank order race/color line/racism came first even regarding the freedom of the two closest women in his life, his wife Nina and daughter Yolande. However, James' designation for Du Bois as profeminist still is appropriate. He is perceptive about the constraints of motherhood and the ways in which societal restrictions placed upon women turn them into housewives instead of enabling them to develop intellectually and produce their best work. He called this the damnation of women. Undoubtedly his insight stems from his own personal experiences with black women, beginning with his relationship with his mother. "The Damnation of Women" centers on the positionality of women in society and include memories of his mother, cousins Inez, Emma, and Ide Fuller as examples of widow, wife, maiden, and white outcast. These women were not self-centered, something for which feminist are criticized. Clenora Hudson-Weems, in defining Africana womanism states that an Africana Womanist is "family-centered" whereas the black feminist is self-centered. Du Bois clearly sees the results of the lack of self-centeredness when he writes of his examples, pointing out that "[T]hey existed not for themselves, but for men; they were named after the men to whom they were related and not after the fashion of their own souls."[4] Human beings first and foremost must exist for themselves. Adult human beings must be self-actualized in order to be fully functioning members of society. Du Bois saw that within the confinement of patriarchal wifehood, motherhood, and single womanhood there was no chance for self-actualizing freedom that comes with equality of opportunity, education, and economic independence. Women must have power and intelligence, Du Bois was convinced. He declared that "[T]his and this only will make the perfect marriage of love and work."[5] Anything less forces women into prostitution; whether as wives who need a husband to support them or as outcasts who walk the streets for money. Du Bois understood the predicament of all women regardless of race or class. Women who escaped were exceptions.

Black women, Du Bois perceived, were "daughters of sorrow" doubly disadvantaged because of sex and race. In the section of "The Damnation of Women" devoted exclusively to the analysis of black women, Du Bois' focuses almost entirely on motherhood, which he romanticizes and contextualizes as the "African mother-idea(l)."[6] But womanhood and motherhood are not identical, as he well knows, for he concluded the essay with homage to strong women and examples of the contributions of women who are not mothers. However, in all of his examples he mentioned none of his peers. James points out that Du Bois quotes from Anna Julia Cooper, although he refers to her only as "one of our women," the anonymity effectively erasing her presence. He also fails to mention the unparalleled antilynching work of Ida B. Wells. Even though Du Bois sees the evils, limits, and illogic of patriarchy, he cannot seem to escape the masculinist framework that presents the male as normative. James argues convincingly that Du Bois has a masculinist worldview; and while he opposed patriarchy and misogyny, he is trapped in the "masculinism [that] can share patriarchy's presupposition of the male as normative without its anti-female rhetoric."[7] Loving paternalism is the result of Du Bois' privileging of his sex, an act not dissimilar to the privileging of race, culture, or sexuality that so often results in domination over whatever group is considered abnormal.

Du Bois' condemnation of the white South for the "wanton and continued and persistent insulting of the black womanhood"[8] is evidence enough of his well-meaning intentions to support and to defend black womanhood. On the other hand, as James observes, it would be shortsighted to overlook the limitations of Du Bois' profeminist position, ones that prevented him from acknowledging the flesh and blood black women intellectuals of his own day who were vocal and politically active. His limitations do not, however, diminish his significant contributions in defending insults from whites as well as from Black male sexists. One instance of white insult was the idea to place a statue of mammy as a tribute to black motherhood. Du Bois denounced the idea as "a perversion of motherhood."[9] He understood the paradox thrust upon black mothers forced to succor white charges.

Characteristically ahead of his time in many respects, he is postmodern in his statements regarding women, and especially black women, as sex objects. In 1920 he writes: "When in this world a man comes forward with a thought, a deed, a vision, we ask not, how does he look—but what is his message? [But] The world still wants to ask that a woman primarily be pretty. . . ."[10] Almost one hundred years have elapsed since his observation and yet the 2008 presidential election, historic and unprecedented in the choice of a black man as commander in chief of the United States, still had people engaged in the sexist rhetoric regarding Sarah Palin's, Michelle Obama's, and Hillary Clinton's dress and physical appearances.

In 1915 Du Bois spoke out on women's right to vote. In response to the argument posed by Kelly Miller, dean at Howard University, who said that women were the weaker sex, capable of rearing children and not much else, Du Bois declared: "[T]he statement that woman is weaker than man is sheer rot: It is the same sort of thing that we hear about 'darker races' and 'lower classes.' Difference, either physical or spiritual, does not argue weakness or inferiority."[11] He attacked the idea of "benevolent guardianship" articulated by those who objected to women voting because they claimed "that everything which women with the ballot might do for themselves can be done for them."[12] This same argument was used to keep blacks disenfranchised. The issue of women's rights formed a part of Du Bois' understanding of a democratic society. True democracy, he argued, is inclusive not exclusive and must be if it is to succeed.

He used the pages of *The Crisis* to argue for women's right to vote and the right to work and the right to pursue a career without having to sacrifice family and motherhood. Du Bois asserted that it was the right of women to choose motherhood at her own discretion. From the pages of *The Crisis*, May 1914, he declared: "In law and in custom our women have no rights which a white man is bound to respect."[13] The law and custom of violence and abuse of black women came from black as well as from white men. By law and custom all men could rape their wives, beat their wives, and in other ways terrorize women. Du

Bois' statement is one that shows clearly the simultane-ity of gender and race for black women. In 1912 arguing facetiously about the "Divine Right"[14] of the white man to seduce black women, he concludes that when Black men kill lecherous whites they should be happy to be lynched. He says it's worth it.

In "The Burden of Black Women," published in 1914, Du Bois again alludes to motherhood as being part of the oppression of women. In the poem "The Black Mother" myth combines with the strong woman image: "Black mother of the iron hills that guard the blazing sea" is also the "married maiden, Mother of God" through which the black Christ must be born—a heavy burden indeed. Clearly, Du Bois sought to replace the besmirched image of black womanhood with a positive albeit romanticized version that superimposes motherhood onto womanhood; at the same time he seems to recognize the woman's innate "soul a-struggling to be free."[15]

While Du Bois has been critiqued for his failure to completely acknowledge his black women peers, usurping black female political agency, [16]he also has been named as one *womanist* forefather, another being Frederick Doug-lass. Gary Lemons employs both the terms *feminist* and *womanist* in his text regarding Du Bois. Since 1983 when Alice Walker introduced the term *womanist* other terms have surfaced or remained intact that complicate mean-ings. The original term *feminist,* which Lemons employs, means pro-woman, that is, a person who argues for the rights and freedom of women.

The thoughts and ideas of early Black feminists were generated from their peculiar experiences as black women. The black women leaders of the early twentieth century were feminists who simultaneously fought against both sexism and racism. In the second wave of the feminism movement that emerged patterning and following the Civil Rights Movement, *feminism* took on unacceptable connotations for many black women. That the movement was racist and led by middle and upper-class white women is undeniable. However, so was the first wave of the feminist movement. Anna Julia Cooper, Mary Church Terrell, Ida B. Wells, Frances Ellen Watkins Harper, and many others, themselves educated black elites, assumed a feminist stance for the cause of black women's rights and freedom. The problem is, as bell hooks and Patricia Hill Collins aptly perceive, that feminism in the 70s came to be associated with lesbianism. On the one hand, some feminists were indeed lesbians. On the other hand, labeling the entire movement "man-hating lesbians" was a ruse to appeal to the homophobic heterosexist beliefs prevalent in black communities. In addition to the prejudices surrounding lesbians, many black women rejected the idea of a self-conscious, self-centered theory of being woman.

During what historian Paula Giddings has named the masculine decade of the 1960s[17] feminists advocated raising oneself before raising children and families. The rhetoric of the Black Power/Black Nationalist/Cultural Nationalist movements preached the dogma of women birthing warriors for the black nation and for the revolution, not of becoming warriors themselves. Women were seen as existing for men, not for themselves. This old-fashioned, Victorian way of contemplating womanhood was undergirded by the Christian church and by the Nation of Islam; the latter was at the height of its popularity during the 1970s.[18] The biblical creation story of woman taken from man, woman as helpmeet, woman as cause for the downfall of man—as temptress, seducer, whore—laid the foundation for misogynistic treatment of and efforts to control women, or perhaps it was misogynistic feelings that created the beliefs. Cultural Nationalist Amiri Baraka in 1970 stated, "we do not believe in equality of men and women . . . we could never be equals . . . nature has not provided thus . . . . we will complement each other."[19] Johnnetta Cole and Beverly Guy-Sheftall compare Baraka's stance to the nineteenth-century Euro-American notion of a benevolent patriarchy based on essentialist notions of gender.

While there were many men who embraced the ideas and attitudes of the past, there were women who also accepted the ideas of patriarchy. Some people embraced the idea that black women were already free. They were free to be beaten, raped, and murdered, but these issues of violence and abuse were not topics for discussion in polite company or otherwise. Considered "dirty linen" not to be aired in public, abuse was shrouded in silence. If women saw themselves as "good Christian wives and mothers" or as "good Muslim wives and mothers" or even if they had been intimidated by the myth of the castrating black matriarch popularized by the Moynihan Report identifying the black family as a "tangle of pathology"[20] and by some black men who believed it, they would reject feminism. Some women, captured by neither religious nor social rhetoric, still found themselves conflicted when asked about feminism. bell hooks observes that like black women of the nineteenth century "contemporary black women felt they were asked to choose between a black movement that primarily served the interests of black male patriarchs and a women's movement which served the interest of racist white women."[21] Some women chose feminism, but as Hooks points out, the vast majority chose to align themselves with black patriarchy in the hope that women's interests would be addressed. However, racism would remain the priority. If we could unravel the mythological theology embedded in the Judeo-Christian dogma, perhaps we could see the metaphysical message in the Genesis allegory—that woman is in man. How else could she be taken from him? That man also is in woman. We all are androgynous—female and male. If we could accept that we are all that is fully human, then we could move beyond the temptation to demonize, marginalize, or reject all that may appear unlike ourselves.

In light of the problems connected with the *F* word, Walker offered *Womanist* that she defined as "a black feminist or feminist of color" and one "who loves other women, sexually and/or nonsexually"—who "appreciates and prefers women's culture. . . . Sometimes loves individual men, sexually and/or nonsexually" and perhaps the most defining feature of her definition, a woman "committed to survival and wholeness of entire people, male *and* female" (emphasis in original). According to Walker's definition, a womanist is "not a separatist" but a "universalist."[22] Walker's definition was rejected by some women who refused any connection with the word *feminist*; so black feminist, which acknowledges the unique angle of vision of black women, still is not acceptable. Daphne Ntiri states that Walker's definition "provokes feelings of alienation from men and evokes lesbian possibilities." Further she states that "[T]he survival and wholeness of the black family appear not to be central to Walker's womanism."[23] Apparently lesbians, gay men, bisexuals and transgendered people and children are not to be considered part of the black family. Ntiri also misreads Patricia Hill Collins when she suggests that Hill Collins and Hudson-Weems are making the same argument regarding how black women define themselves. Quoted out of context it might appear that Hill Collins is saying that those black women who identify with feminism must be recorded as being either non-black or less authentically black; however, what she is saying is describing the narrowness of labels. The context of the quotation is this: "When given these two narrow and false choices, [black feminist or feminist] black women routinely choose 'race' and let the lesser question of 'gender' go."[24] The message in Hill Collins' article is twofold. In analyzing labels, Walker's womanist and black feminist, she finds value in both; Walker's for its inclusive and multiple definitions and black feminist for its power to disrupt "racism inherent in presenting feminism as a for-whites-only ideology and political movement." The term black feminist declares that white women are not the only feminist and not the normative feminist.[25]

Hill Collins also suggests, as did Du Bois, that it is time to move beyond the level of definition, and certainly the time has arrived to move beyond the issue of who is or who is not "authentically" black. In March 1928, Roland A. Barton, a high school sophomore, wrote to Du Bois at *The Crisis* to ask why black people were referred to as Negroes instead of just plain Americans. He said that Negro was "a white man's word." Du Bois' response is instructive. He said "Do not . . . make the all too common error of mistaking names for things. Names are only conventional signs for identifying things. Things are the reality that counts. If a thing is despised, either because of ignorance or because it is despicable, you will not alter matters by changing its name." Du Bois concluded that we could just as easily call ourselves "Cheiropolidi" for all the difference it would make regarding the problems that we face.

The argument of some Afrocentrists[26] is that Black people need to work together in order to overthrow racist capitalist systems and, Aldridge might add, in order to also understand Judeo-Christian dogma. Under ideal circumstances I would agree. However, here is why we cannot wait. There is no indication that the masses of black people in the United States even want to disassemble the current economic system not to mention reject Judeo-Christian precepts. Some black people even believe that we have now arrived at a postracist or postracial society. Meanwhile, black women cannot wait for the real demise of racism or the death of capitalism. Issues of safety and health for black women of all stripes including lesbians and bisexuals need addressing now. Hill Collins' statement is worth quoting. She insists that "[R]acism is a gender specific phenomenon, and Black antiracist politics that do not make gender central are doomed to fail."[27] Another reason posited for rejecting feminism is that it increases "tension in the already strained interpersonal atmosphere in which black men and women interact,"[28] a reason reminiscent of the argument articulated by many southern whites regarding civil and human rights for black people. The idea that feminism derives solely from white women is little different from the charge that the Civil Rights Movement was Communist led and inspired. Nevertheless, to avoid the idea of feminism altogether, Africana womanism, distinct from Walker's womanism, offers an alternative that to my way of thinking is too proscriptive and grounded in Black Nationalist philosophy of female self-sacrifice and other stereotypical behaviors. It aligns too closely with the nineteenth century "Cult of True Womanhood." Hill Collins is correct in asserting that no term currently exists that adequately represents the diverse politics and positions of all Black women.

Womanist, Alice Walker's version, which Lemons uses to describe both Douglass and Du Bois, has been further complicated by its adoption by black women theologians. Monica Coleman captures the dilemma when she writes:

> Perhaps it is the political edge that draws me toward the label "black feminist." The word *feminist* still conjures images of commitments I express on a daily basis—issues around music, love, and teaching . . . When I tell my black male friends that I'm a womanist, they think of me as a black churchwoman . . . When I tell them that I am a black feminist, they get a little uneasy, because they start to wonder if I'm aligned with lesbians, if I'm going to question their power, and if I am going to call God "She"—all of which I do.[29]

The word feminist has the disruptive effect that Coleman desires—the power to call into question preconceived assumptions regarding sex and gender. Ironically, black women theologians have made use of Walker's term without fully embracing its complete meaning. They, like the Afrocentrists, have not been completely open to diversity regarding sexual orientation.

Lemons' analysis of Du Bois combines the political edge of feminism with Walker's womanism, and at times he uses the terms interchangeably. Du Bois falls short of being a Walker-defined womanist, for he too is trapped in the Victorian attitude of heteronormative masculinity. Lemons, recognizing Du Bois' shortcomings, still is able to see as progressive Du Bois' efforts to support women's rights. Nevertheless, his close critical reading of Du Bois' essay about his daughter's wedding, "So the Girl Marries," is telling. That is, it exposes the limitations or blind spots, if you will, of what Lemons calls the "feminist father."[30] In the essay, as Lemons points out, Du Bois undermines the power of his wife as mother by silencing her voice and by taking control of the education and development of their daughter. Lemons writes that Du Bois' "feminist ideas of black womanhood and mothering . . . relegate Nina to a trivial role, making her only a surrogate for the true mother—Du Bois himself."[31] Lemons argues convincingly that Du Bois idealized black womanhood and saw in Yolande the perfect ideal "modern black woman." Du Bois begins the essay with the admission that he was startled when he became the father of a girl. He admits, too, that Nina was stuck with the boring job of chaperoning Yolande. Du Bois slips into a masculinist paradigm when he says, "But Mother stuck to her job. I've always had the feeling that the real trick was turned in those years, by a very soft-voiced and persistent Mother who was always hanging about unobtrusively . . . . Father, of course, was busy with larger matters and weightier problems, including himself." [32] Du Bois, acting as "father knows best" gave instructions that both wife and daughter obeyed.

Yolande Du Bois and Countee Cullen's wedding was the talk of Harlem, and well it should have been. Not only was it an extravagant display, it was, as Lemons insists and as Du Bois himself admits, "the symbolic march of young and black America."[33] If Du Bois orchestrated the wedding of his daughter to Cullen, and nothing in the essay suggests that he did, one can only wonder why, given Cullen's sexual orientation.[34] Despite all the pomp and circumstance, the marriage would fail. Lewis writes that for all of Du Bois' defense of the rights of women, his essay on birth control, and his stance on abstract gender rights, he "serenely arrogated the right to decide the fate of two young people whose intrinsic emotional needs he willfully, myopically resolved not to understand . . . he succumbed to a tyranny that resulted in the symbolic and literal immolation of his own flesh and blood in the service of genetic, gendered, classist, and racial fantasies."[35] When it becomes clear that the marriage is in trouble, Du Bois blames its failure on his daughter. As Mason Stokes points out, Du Bois, in a letter to Countee Cullen, says that Yolande is "spoiled . . . does not know what she wants or loves or hopes for"[36]; and to her he says that she should not distract her husband but help him to become a better poet for the world to acknowledge. Du Bois summarily dismisses his daughter's concerns.

Theory and practice often cause problems for those under public scrutiny. Du Bois is no exception. His relationship with and description of his wife and daughter might undermine his prowomanist stance were it not for his own recognition of his shortcomings. Lemons says although Du Bois recognized his wife's loneliness, he failed to comprehend his role in her predicament. I would argue that he did indeed recognize his role in it. In the eulogy for his wife, an essay published in *The Chicago Globe*, July 15, 1950, titled "I Bury My Wife," Du Bois admitted that he was not a good husband. Lewis called him a "priapic adulterer."[37] Du Bois says that "[T]he family and its interests were never the main center of [his] life" and describes his wife of fifty-five years as a housewife, one who could not forget her housework and "romp and laugh." It is quite possible that even if given the opportunity to escape the drudgery of housework and join her husband in his intellectual pursuits, she might not have wanted to do so. She might have felt complete. Lewis however points to her correspondence, which reveals what he calls "a sad record of psychosomatic debility and shriveling superego."[38] Her letters also reveal her desire to be with her husband and his insistence on them living apart for the purpose of educating the daughter as he saw fit; and again, when he returned to Atlanta University alone and insisted that Nina remain in New York. If Nina Gomer's life in the great shadow of Du Bois does not fit well with his profeminist stance, his second wife, Shirley Graham—even more than his daughter—is the ideal modern woman. Intelligent, well educated, economically independent, well traveled, and worldly, Shirley Graham Du Bois was also politically astute.

As for Yolande, when her second marriage began to disintegrate Du Bois at first reprimanded her for being selfish and not trying to communicate with her husband, Arnett Williams. However, soon it was discovered that Williams was an abusive man who drank too much. Calling Du Bois an early feminist father-in-law, Lewis quotes from the letter to Williams: "You seem to think that [marriage] involves complete physical ownership of the woman, and her utter subjection to your wishes at all times."[39] Had Yolande been permitted by her class-conscious father to marry the man she loved, jazz saxophonist Jimmie Lunceford, she might have found happiness in a stable marriage and avoided two divorces. Instead, both Lewis and Lemons charge that Du Bois ruled his family like a benevolent despot. The self-autonomy Du Bois granted his women characters in fiction, apparently were withheld from Nina and Yolande. Following his directions did not lead to their self-empowerment.

Cheryl Townsend Gilkes, writing about Du Bois, emphasizes that his writings acknowledge the social and political significance of women. She points to his early works as a reporter for the *New York Globe*, where he wrote about the activities of the women in the church sewing circle. At Fisk Du Bois continued to write, first as exchange editor of the *Fisk Herald*, where in 1885 he wrote, "The column on woman's work is interesting and a first rate woman's rights argument."[40] As editor of the Fisk publication in December 1887, Du Bois published his first novella, *Tom Brown at Fisk*, in which Ella Boyd, an educated and economically independent student-teacher inspires Tom to become a credit to his race and obtain an education. Du Bois' opening sentence, "It's hard to be a woman, but a black one—!"[41] reveals his sensitivity to the plight of Black women and aligns him with progressive black women like Josephine St.Pierre Ruffin, suffragist and founder of the Women's Era Club. Gilkes notes that Ruffin employed Du Bois while he was a student at Harvard. He published his Harvard daily themes in her weekly newspaper *The Courant*.

On the pages of *The Crisis*, in various newspapers, in his autobiographical writings, and in his fiction Du Bois stands for social justice and for freedom. He argues that "no nation, race, or sex, has a monopoly of ability or ideas."[42] *The Quest for the Silver Fleece* is a novel for the "Darker Sisters" according to Lemons. In the character of Zora Creswell, Du Bois idealizes black womanhood in terms of the woman's self-sacrifice; however, he also enables Zora to become self-actualized. Nellie McKay reads the novel as a "black female *Bildungsroman*" and reveals that unlike the literary white heroine who struggles to become self-conscious, then finding no use for her talents goes insane or commits suicide, the black female who develops into what Du Bois called efficient womanhood, can assume the role of social leader for her race.

As with the other issues that Du Bois raised regarding Black Studies, the concerns he voiced about women are present today in Black Women's Studies. Black Studies professor Laverne Gyant[43] echoes Du Bois' concerns when she identifies balancing the personal and professional as an issue for black women today. The need for Black Women's Studies is just as clear as was the need for Black Studies. Too many, certainly not all, Black men practice the same kind of exclusionary tactics as their white colleagues had exercised prior to the birth of Black Studies. Kelly Miller was not alone in his outmoded idea of the role of women. Many black nationalists carried the tradition into the late twentieth century. Therefore while women like Delores Aldridge, Carlene Young, Johnella Butler, Vivian Gordon, Adelaide Gulliver, and too many more to name have worked tirelessly in the vineyard establishing Black Studies in higher education, men have tended to drink the wine of their sweat, gaining both visibility and credibility.

Gyant believes that the tendency to gloss over black women's contributions to the field is changing and offers for support the chapter on women in the revised edition of Karenga's *Introduction to Black Studies*. What probably is more significant than the inclusion of women in a textbook chapter is the education of a cadre of Women's Studies scholars to continue the tradition black women have established in the field of Black Studies. The Africana Women's Studies Program at Clark Atlanta University founded by Shelby Lewis offers both the masters and doctoral degrees. Founded in 1982, this program is the only one of its kind. Interestingly, the founding of Clark Atlanta's program coincided with the publication of the groundbreaking book *All the Women Are White, All the Men Are Black, But Some of Us Are Brave*.[44] Another important development is the Women's Research and Resource Center at Spelman College founded in 1981 by Beverly Guy-Sheftall, which now offers both a major and minor in Women's Studies. The recent publication of *Still Brave: The Evolution of Black Women's Studies*[45] talks back to the seminal book that called attention to the failure of both Women's Studies and Black Studies in addressing black women's issues.

The message clearly is as it was for the development of Black Studies; black women are their own best advocates. However, not all Black Studies scholars agree that black women require separate study. The sociologist and founding director of the African and African American Studies Program established in 1971 at Emory University, Delores Aldridge, believes that integrating studies by and about women into the general Africana Studies curriculum is most desirable. She states that "black women who focus on the overall black experience are as important as those who focus solely on women."[46] In "Towards Integrating Africana Womanism into Africana Studies," Aldridge observes that the National Council for Black Studies has revised its core curriculum to include women. She acknowledges that there continues to be a dearth of courses that focus on black women; and when they do, she writes, "Most often the courses are in literature occasionally tied to a family course."[47] There are exceptions, but she notes that these exceptions usually are taught by "proactive Africana Women's scholars."[48] Issues regarding Black Women's Studies are quite similar to the ones that plagued Black Studies.[49]

Elizabeth Cole and Nesha Haniff outline the problems that a separate field of Black Women Studies faces. Beginning with the 1989 Barbara Christian quotation that black women have no "home really fitted to our needs" because "the study of women of color is itself a critique of Afro-American studies and of Women'[s] Studies,"[50] Cole and Haniff recognize the precarious position that both Black Studies and Women's Studies occupy in the academy. Neither field is as solidly based as more traditional disciplines. Given the politics of scarcity and declining institutional support, it is easy to understand how some African American studies scholars might see Black Women's Studies as divisive. More fundamental than economic resources are what Cole and Haniff describe as "deep fissures" that exist within the discipline.[51] They reference Alan Colon's historical outline of the intellectual roots of Black Studies. The main distinctions include:

> scholars working in the tradition of Carter G. Woodson, and the black cultural nationalists and from these come the Traditionalist and Afrocentrist. Traditionalists tend to remain within traditional disciplines, history is one example, and to focus their work on Black people in the United States and the Diaspora. Afrocentrists reject traditional disciplines because they are steeped in Eurocentric ways of knowing. Afrocentrists focus on "African-centered epistemologies."[52]

Given these paradigms, Cole and Haniff are correct to question the place of Black Women's Studies within Black Studies.

Black Women's Studies within the context of the Afrocentric paradigm of Black Studies is represented in Aldridge and Young's *Out of the Revolution*. However, within this volume, Cole and Haniff point out that the place for feminism is foreclosed. The rationale for the rejection of feminism is articulated in Gordon's chapter that frames "both feminism and sexism as originating in European thought."[53] In order for Black Women's Studies to become part of Black Studies, Cole and Haniff argue that women would have to accept the idea of gender complementarity thought to be necessary for "intellectual and political power."[54] They concede that "the argument laid out by Aldridge and her colleagues supports the centrality of women to the black studies project,"[55] which is more than can be said for the traditionalists. Therefore, scholars that reject the Africana Womanism model within the Afrocentric paradigm find themselves almost by default in the field of Women's Studies.

Among traditionalist, gender issues, if and when they are addressed, place third following concerns of race and class. Hill Collins notes that gender issues of neither black women nor black men have received any sustained attention in Afrocentrism either.[56] In some ways gender is thought to belong to women just as race belonged only to those who were nonwhite. Black scholars who challenge the prevailing paradigms in Black Studies and embrace a feminist posture face the question raised by Christian in 1988: "But Who Do You Really Belong To—Black Studies or Women's Studies?"[57] This question has yet to be answered. The position of black feminist scholars having feet in both camps is not necessarily disadvantageous. Du Bois, in writing "The Souls of White Folk,"[58] recognized the unusual vantage point of a particular distance. In his case the distance was race—but for black women it is both race and gender at once as we can view both Black Studies and Women's Studies "undressed and from the back and side."[59] From such a position black feminist and Womanist criticism can break new ground.

Du Bois paid homage to black women in 1907 when he published the poems "The Burden of Black Women" in *The Horizon*; and when he published "The Black Mother," "Hail Columbia," and "Woman Suffrage," in *The Crisis*. An article, "Sex and Racism," appeared in *The Independent* in 1957 and is listed in the Lewis *Reader* under Women's Rights, although it has nothing to do with women in particular. Du Bois' publications, including "So the Girl Marries" and "I Bury My Wife," reveal his profeminist consciousness. These writings are not the sum total of his focus on black women. Barbara McCaskill[60] writes that Du Bois challenged the assumption that black women belonged only in the home and not in the public sphere. In *The Souls of Black Folk* he acknowledged Phillis Wheatley's contribution to the arts as well as Frances Harper's and Gertrude Mossell's activism, and he helped to promote the women writers of the Harlem Renaissance. Further, McCaskill says, "Had twentieth-century scholars read more Du Bois, they perhaps would have noted his recognition of Linda Brent . . . as an African American slave narrator."[61] Black women would have garnered more recognition in the Black Studies Movement as well. The women who were Du Bois' contemporaries and peers included not only Anna Julia Cooper and Mary Church Terrell, but also Adella Hunt Logan, the first librarian at Tuskegee, and Ida B. Wells Barnett, a crusader against lynching. There are many others. To be sure, Du Bois paid respect to women's contributions while at the same time adhering to an essentialist and homogenized view of black womanhood. Ironically, that view of black womanhood is still prevalent today in sectors of Black Studies.

Another movement is afoot within the purview of Black Studies, and that is the issue of gender and sexuality. Du Bois, in his wide-ranging and prophetic vision has even provided guidance in what appears to be still another variation in the complex tangle of race. *Darkwater*, appropriately titled for the murky waters of the soul, the subconscious—the Jungian collective unconsciousness—offers an allegorical rendering of gender and sexuality. Often read in terms of its political context of racism and imperialism, it can also be understood for the metaphysical aspects of oneness that it suggests. The allegorical section titled "The Princess of the Hither Isles" offers one example of a gendered opening, one that Du Bois himself might never have intended; but such is the results of exploring dark water. Characters, the princess, the King of Yonder Kingdom, and the beggars are aspects of the same self. The "Leap!" of Du Bois' penultimate line becomes an integration of all the disparate parts. Black Studies and Black Women's Studies of the twenty-first century must make the leap from the traps of racism, capitalism, imperialism, but also from outmoded ideas of masculinity and femininity.

In 1906 Du Bois proclaimed, "Either the United States will destroy ignorance, or ignorance will destroy the United States."[62] The summary of Du Bois' contributions demonstrates his effort to eradicate ignorance with regard to the life and experiences of black people. Writing in *Phylon* in 1983, W.J. Lange stated that not only should Du Bois be remembered as the "foremost pioneer" of Black Studies, he should also be acknowledged as one of the founders of American social science.[63] Yet this was not the case when I began this study in 1982. During part of Du Bois' lifetime his works enjoyed immense popularity, especially *The Souls of Black Folk*; and he was able to publish his writings, often receiving both favorable and unfavorable reviews by the critics. After the Communist scare of the McCarthy Era, however, his popularity and ability to publish his works were greatly diminished. Following his death in 1963 there was a steady but small group of scholars who continued to reference his works in learned journals. The *Index to Book Reviews in Humanities Journals 1802–1974* mentions his works forty times. Previously Du Bois had not enjoyed the normal recognition and/or attention accorded a scholar of his stature. For example, he is not nearly so widely known for giving birth to Black Studies in higher education as say Melville Herskovits is for beginning African Studies. Despite his pioneering work in social sciences and his fathering of black urban sociology, he is not as recognized as Emile Durkheim or Carl Rogers in psychology, or as B.F. Skinner is in terms of his learning theory.

Lange (1983) identified two conditions that continue to obstruct the full recognition of Du Bois. First, persistent discipline territorialism among American social scientists makes it difficult to categorize accurately and properly any profound cross-disciplinary scholar, Du Bois, for example. The other condition is found in American society and is primarily responsible for denying Du Bois his rightful place among the fathers of American sociology and anthropology. Du Bois was a black man who became a Marxist. He also was a Pan-Africanist and civil rights leader. His vision and scholarship knew no provincial bounds. None of these positions has ever found full acceptance or recognition in American higher education, let alone in American society.

Even among his own people Du Bois was often under-utilized. Fortunately, this appears to be changing with the flurry of publications surrounding the centennial of *The Souls of Black Folk* and the publication of the Oxford Du

Bois, a series by Oxford University Press, edited by Henry Louis Gates, Jr., that reprints Du Bois' works for a new generation of students and scholars. The great debate over Black Studies was in part due to the limited access to Du Bois' works. At the 1969 symposium on Black Studies held at Yale University many issues were discussed, issues that Du Bois had dealt with in his many books and articles. Yet his name was not mentioned, and his works were not cited. A review of the plans for Black Studies at Berkeley reveals the same thing with reference to quoting and citing Du Bois. In one course, Sociology 191R (Sociology of the Black Family), a reading list of fifteen books was required. Not one book authored or edited by Du Bois was on the list. The workshop on Black Studies at the Institute of the Black World in Atlanta in 1969 had historian Vincent Harding advocating "his" idea for an "International Center for Black Studies." Harding suggested forming a consortium with the Atlanta Center, Fisk, Shaw, and Howard. He did not mention Du Bois' efforts in this area.

One result of the Black Studies movement has been an effort on the part of society at large to rectify the exclusion of black Americans from the educational media resulting in the production of posters and various other print media (flash cards) that include the biographies of famous Black Americans. In a poster by Nabisco, great black educators are listed, among them Booker T. Washington; however, once again, Du Bois is not listed. The 1983 Miller High Life Calendar lists Civil Rights Leaders, and while Paul Robeson is included, W.E.B. Du Bois is not. Between 1965 and 1970, the height of the Black Studies movement, the *Cumulative Index to Periodical Literature* (March 1959– February 1970) lists thirty-nine articles on the issues of Black Studies. Not one article refers to Du Bois in its title and not one of those same articles examined for this study (twenty-four) referred to or acknowledged Du Bois' theory or concept of Black Studies. This is not to say that during the movement Du Bois was never mentioned or quoted, but it is to insist that it did not happen to the extent that it should have.

Du Bois' works between the period 1896–1910 were seminal to the development of Black Studies. His writings challenged the "scientific racism" of the day, the social Darwinism and eugenics movements that maintained the inferiority of black people. Du Bois, through his research and in his writings, pointed out absurdities in the scientific methodology of the researchers who sought to document the inferiority of blacks; and while his reasoning and research predate the term, it laid the foundation for what is now Black Studies.

His writings were significant to its development because he demanded that the studies be truly scientific. In 1903 Du Bois wrote:

> We seldom study the condition of the Negro to-day honestly and carefully. It is so much easier to assume that we know it all. Or perhaps, having already reached conclusions in our own minds, we are loath to have them disturbed by facts. And yet how little we really know of these million,—of their daily lives and longings, of their homely joys and sorrows, of their real shortcomings and the meaning of their crimes![64]

Du Bois' demand for Black Studies came years before others joined in and advocated the studies. He called for a comprehensive anthropometrical study of black Americans several years before Franz Boas and other anthropologists made similar pleas.[65] Du Bois demanded truth, and his writings during this period demonstrate his efforts to search for truth. On his twenty-fifth birthday while still a student in Germany, he wrote, "Be the truth what it may I will seek it on the pure assumption that it is worth seeking—And Heaven nor Hell, God nor Devil, shall turn me from my purpose till I die."[66] Melodramatic, perhaps, but his writings were trendsetting and his vision prophetic. In his contributions to Black Studies, Du Bois was both a participant and an observer. As a social scientist he observed the black experience and reported what he saw. As a black man he lived the black experience and through that experience he created his prolific works.

In the Atlanta University Studies Du Bois referred to African survivals a good fifty years before Melville Herskovits's *Myth of the Negro Past* presented the thesis on African survivals in African American culture. Du Bois anticipated many of the questions that black students and scholars were to face in the late 1960s when they began to demand Black Studies programs. On the question of subject matter, Du Bois' contributions alone offer ample material on nearly every subject covered in Black Studies. On the issue of politics he stressed scientific accuracy and avoided ideological biases. However, he did believe that all ideological points of view should be examined and studied, and that the analysis of politics or any other politically motivated ideology should be undertaken in the university.

In terms of standard curriculum, Du Bois saw Black Studies as an interdisciplinary field of study, but he wanted to allow great latitude in order not to inhibit creative approaches to the studies. On the charge of reverse racism, Du Bois recognized the speciousness of this argument and correctly predicted that it would be forthcoming. He said separatism was necessary for the growth and development of the field because of the racist society in which Black people were forced to function. Finally, in terms of marketability, Du Bois perhaps never envisioned a degree exclusively in Black Studies. Nonetheless, in his address "Careers Open to College-Bred Negroes" he distinguished between education and training. Black Studies would logically fall under the heading of education. He pointed to a variety of fields open to educated people.

As a young man, Du Bois believed that education was the cure for racism, for he assumed that if people knew better they would do better. He believed that the scientific study would reveal truth, that ignorance caused prejudice, and that through knowledge people would see the error of their ways and alter their behavior. He also believed that self-knowledge, which would be gained or enhanced through the scientific study of the black experience, would instill racial pride and promote self-esteem in young black students whose history and culture were either ignored or demeaned in American education.

Du Bois' education and life experiences formed the basis of his values and philosophical beliefs. He spent over twenty years of his life obtaining a formal education. Consequently, he valued education and believed it would make a difference in the way society functioned. He thought the by-products of education were altruism and liberalism, not selfishness, sexism, and racism; life experiences, however, taught him the former was the exception rather than the rule. Therefore, as he matured, he tried to combine his intellectual idealism with the politics of protest and agitation, recognizing that knowledge of a problem was not always enough to produce a solution. Education and travel produced in Du Bois a *Weltanschauung* that few others shared. In examining a problem he was able to see its national and international ramifications.

As an old man, Du Bois never stopped searching for the solution to the problems of race. He understood the complexity of race, class, color, and gender and did not believe as he once had that they could be solved by democracy, at least not as democracy was practiced in the United States.

Du Bois' concrete contributions are preserved in books, pamphlets, poems, and speeches. The many journal articles, newspaper columns, collected papers, and letters present a repository of information on the black experience in the United States and abroad and show the evolution of a black American intellectual who spent all of his adult life in the quest of the silver fleece for freedom and peace.

Notes

Introduction

1. Allen, 1974; Cleveland, 1969; Genovese, 1969.
2. Turner, 1980
3. Ibid., 52.
4. Foner, 1970.
5. Marable, in L.R. and J.A. Gordon, Eds., 2006, 96.
6. Gordon, 98.
7. In Green and Driver, Eds., 1978, 80.
8. In Foner, 1970, 48.

Chapter 1

1. Lewis, 1993.
2. Du Bois, 1968.
3. Du Bois, Memorial Park, 1979.
4. Du Bois, 1968, 62.
5. Ibid.
6. Ibid., 71.
7. Ibid., 73
8. Lewis, 1993, 29.
9. R. McGrawville, *Dictionary of American Negro Biography* (New York: Norton, 1982).

10. A.R. Mayo, "Charles Lewis Reason." *Negro History Bulletin* 5 (June 1942): 212-15.
11. Ballard, [2004] 1974. *Education of Black Folk.*
12. Lawson and Merrill, 1984.
13. *See:* Moore, 2003.
14. Du Bois, 1968, 74-75.
15. Ibid., 74.
16. Ibid., 75.
17. Du Bois, 1968.
18. Lacy, 1970.
19. Du Bois, 1968, 21.
20. *Encyclopedia Americana,* 1983, 830 and *Encyclopedia Britannica*, on-line ed., s.v. "far east."
21. Wells, 1971.
22. Du Bois, 1968.
23. Harding, 1980, 65.
24. Bergman, 1969.
25. Bailey, 1966.
26. Bergman, 1969.
27. Ibid., 278.
28. Ibid.
29. Bailey, 1966, 425. *See also* Kelley and Lewis, 2000.
30. Ibid.
31. Ibid.
32. Du Bois, 1968, 79.
33. Ibid.
34. Lewis, 1994, 53.
35. Du Bois, 1920.
36. Du Bois, 1968.
37. Ibid., 83.
38. Du Bois, 1968, 108.
39. Ibid., 183.
40. Ibid., 108.
41. Ibid., 110.
42. Ibid., 108.

43. *Fisk University Catalog*, 1888.
44. Du Bois, 1968, 112.
45. Ibid.
46. Lewis, 1994, 72.
47. Ibid., 73.
48. Du Bois, 1968, 122.
49. Report of the Pan-African Conference, July 23-25, 1900, at Westminster, London, 10-12. Also in Lewis, 1993, 639.
50. Du Bois, 1968, 132.
51. Ibid.
52. Ibid., 133.
53. Ibid., 146.
54. Ibid.
55. Ibid., 126.
56. Ibid., 148.
57. Marable, 1986, 16.
58. Du Bois, 1968.
59. Ibid.
60. Ibid., 154.
61. Ibid., 157.
62. Ibid.
63. Ibid.

CHAPTER 2

1. Du Bois, 1898, in Provenzo, Jr., 2002, 86.
2. Ibid.
3. Ibid., 80.
4. Ibid.
5. Bell, 1997, 110.
6. Baldwin, [1955] 1984, 164.
7. Du Bois, 1898, 86.
8. Ibid.
9. Ibid., 86.

10. Kent State University Library, Special Collections, Campus Strike Papers, 1965-1972, Box 14. Fisk University, January 1970. www.kent.edu/ (accessed October 6, 2009).
11. In Provenzo, Jr., 2002, 83.
12. Ibid., 75.
13. In Lewis, 1994, 538.
14. Du Bois, in Lewis, Ed., 1995, 48-53.
15. Andrews, 1985, 27.
16. Anderson, 1988, 34.
17. Du Bois, 1968, 192.
18. Ibid.
19. Ibid.
20. Lester, 1971.
21. Du Bois, 1968, 197.
22. Ibid., 198.
23. Ibid., 200.
24. Ibid., 1940, 32.
25. Ibid., 1968, 206.
26. Lester, 1971.
27. Du Bois, 1968, 213.
28. Ibid., 1895, in Aptheker, *The Correspondence of W.E.B. Du Bois*, 1973, 39.
29. Randall, [1952] 1967.
30. Du Bois, 1940, 55.
31. *See* Bauerlein, 2004.
32. Aptheker, 1973, *The Correspondence*, 4.
33. Bauerlein, 2004.
34. Du Bois, 1940, 38.
35. Ibid.
36. Lacy, 1970, 60.
37. Washington, 1901.
38. J.H. Franklin, 1965.
39. Du Bois, 1903, 40, in Gates and Oliver, Eds.,1999. Also in J.H. Franklin, 1965, 12.
40. Ibid.

41. Du Bois, 1898.
42. Ibid., 1903, 40.
43. Ibid., 1940, 87.
44. Bauerlein, 2004; Du Bois, 1940.
45. Ibid., 1940, 92.
46. Ibid.
47. Washington, 1896, "The Awakening," n.p.; from www.atlantic.com/ (accessed October 12, 2009).
48. Ibid.
49. Du Bois, 1902. *Atlantic,* 287-97. Also in *Souls,* 1903, 65, in Gates and Oliver, 1999.
50. Du Bois, quoted in McGill, *Atlantic Monthly* 216, no. 5 (1965): 48-81.
51. McGill, 1965.
52. Lacy, 1970, 49.
53. Anderson, 1978.
54. Aldridge, 2008, 15.
55. McGill, 1965.
56. Ibid.
57. Lacy, 1970, 48.
58. Du Bois, 1912, "I am Resolved," *Crisis* (January) 113; quoted in Walden, 61.
59. McGill interview, 1965.
60. Foner, 1970, 28.
61. Du Bois, 1968, 136.
62. Lester, 1971, 208.
63. Du Bois, 1968, 343.
64. J.H. Franklin, 1948.
65. J.H. Franklin, 1965.
66. Du Bois, 1968, 343.
67. Moon, 1972.
68. Contee, 1974.
69. Lacy, 1970.
70. Rudwick, 1960.
71. Du Bois, 1968.

72. Lester, 1971.
73. Ibid., 205.
74. Du Bois, 1919, 7.
75. Lester, 1971.
76. Du Bois, 1921, 5.
77. Ibid., 1919, 166.
78. Lacy, 1970.
79. Ibid., 66.
80. Franklin, 1948; Bergman, 1969.
81. Lacy, 1970, 66.
82. Ibid., 67.
83. Du Bois, 1920, 11.
84. Ibid., 12.
85. Ibid., 1921, 58.
86. Lacy, 1970. *See also* C.B. James, 2009.
87. Du Bois, 1920, 166.
88. Ibid., 1968, 136.
89. Ibid., 1957, quoted in Horne, 1986, 313.
90. Ibid.
91. Ibid.
92. Ibid., 1958.
93. Ibid., 1968, 304.
94. Ibid.
95. Ibid., 1961.
96. Ibid., 1907.
97. Lester, 1971.
98. In Aptheker, 1973. *The Education of Black People*, 81.
99. Du Bois, 1968.
100. Ibid.
101. Ibid.
102. Ibid., 119 published in 5 *Freedomways* 1 (winter): 117-124.
103. Ibid., 1965, 118.
104. Letter to Gus Hall, 1961, in Aptheker, 1978, v.3, 439.
105. Lacy, 1970.
106. Ibid.

107. Von Eschen, 1977; Lacy, 1970.

108. Lacy, 1970, 106.

109. Ibid., 107.

110. Ibid.

111. Ibid.

112. Du Bois, 1968.

113. Ibid.

114. Lacy, 1970, 107.

115. Marable, 1998, 121.

116. Letter to William Foley, in Aptheker, 1978 v.3, 309.

117. Du Bois, 1968.

118. Ibid.

119. Du Bois, 1968, 364.

120. Ibid., 366.

121. Ibid.

122. Ibid.

123. Ibid.

124. Ibid.

125. Du Bois, S.G. 1971.

126. Du Bois, 1968.

127. Ibid., 1968, 395.

128. Ibid.

129. Interview with author, Fisk University, 1987.

130. Du Bois, 1968.

131. Ibid.

132. Du Bois, 1897, 199.

133. Ibid.

134. Ibid., 1968, 11.

135. Ibid., 12.

136. Ibid.

137. Ibid., 21.

138. Ibid.

139. Du Bois, S.G., 1971.

140. *Journal of Modern African Studies,* 2 (1964): 444-47.

141. Du Bois, 1968, 43.

142. Ibid.

143. Ibid., 57-58.

144. Ibid., 361.

145. Ibid.

146. Du Bois, S.G., 1971.

147. Broderick, 1958, 29.

148. Du Bois, S.G., 1971, 229.

149. D.G Du Bois interview with author, 1987.

150. Du Bois, 1968.

151. Du Bois, S.G., 1971, 353.

152. Ibid.

CHAPTER 3

1. Douglass, 1881, in [database on-line] Cornell.edu/ (accessed on October 2, 2009).

2. Du Bois, 1940.

3. Ibid.

4. United States Bureau of Labor Bulletin, 1898, The Negroes of Farmville, Virginia. The Virginia study was edited by W.E.B. Du Bois, Ph.D.

5. Du Bois, 1898, "The Study of the Negro Problems;" 1-23.

6. Du Bois, 1928.

7. Du Bois, 1898, 67.

8. Ibid., 38.

9. Grossman, 1974, 17.

10. Du Bois, 1899, *Bulletin of the Department of Labor*, 4.

11. Du Bois, 1899, 409.

12. Ibid.

13. Du Bois, 1901.

14. Thom, 1901.

15. Laws, 1902.

16. Ibid., 120.

17. Du Bois, 1901.

18. Ibid., 1940.

19. Ibid., 1906.
20. Ibid., 1968, 202.
21. Ibid., 203.
22. Lester, 1971, 187.
23. Ibid., 225.
24. Ibid., 226.
25. Ibid.
26. Ibid., 227.
27. Du Bois, 1968, 206.
28. Ibid.
29. Lester, 1971.
30. Atlanta University Studies available in the Woodruff Library of Clark Atlanta University and on line at http://www.library. umass.edu/specialcoll/digital/dubois/(accessed October 12, 2009).
31. Lester, 1971.
32. Law, 2007, 21.
33. Study no. 3, Du Bois, 1898, 43.
34. Aptheker, 1973; Lewis, 1994.
35. Study no. 5, 34.
36. Study no. 7, 177.
37. Study no. 8, 208.
38. Study no. 12, 1.
39. Du Bois, 1968.
40. Ibid., 216.
41. Ibid.
42. Lester, 1971.
43. Taylor, C.M. 1981; Lester, 1971.
44. Du Bois, 1968.
45. Ibid., 222.
46. Du Bois, 1897, 73.
47. Ibid., 25.
48. Ibid., 1897, 75.
49. Ibid., 1897, 97.
50. Du Bois, 189, 24.

51. Du Bois, 1898, 236.
52. Ibid.
53. Allport, 1954, xi.
54. Ibid.
55. Ibid.
56. Ashley-Montagu, 1997, 100.
57. Du Bois, 1898, 215.
58. Ibid., 242.
59. Du Bois, 1898.
60. Du Bois, 1898, 244.
61. Morais, 1967, 32.
62. Du Bois, 1898, 21.
63. Ibid.
64. Ibid.
65. Ibid., 23.
66. Ibid.
67. Du Bois, 1935, in Provenzo, Jr., ed., 2002, 133.
68. Ibid., 138.
69. Ibid.
70. Ibid., 140.
71. Ibid.
72. Ibid. 141.
73. Du Bois, 1968, 415.
74. Du Bois, 1936, 416.
75. Du Bois, 1933, 181.
76. Ibid., 186.
77. Du Bois, 1933, 573.
78. Ibid., 573.
79. Du Bois, 1933, n.p. *See also* "The Negro College," *Crisis* 40 (August):1933.
80. Du Bois, 1968.
81. Ibid., 130.
82. Du Bois, 1942; 1968.
83. Du Bois, 1968, 313-14.
84. Ibid., 314.

85. Ibid., 314.
86. Ibid., 313.
87. Ibid., 314-17.
88. Ibid.

CHAPTER 4

1. Kilson, 1969, 327.
2. Ibid.
3. C.E. Wilson 1969; Allen, 1974.
4. Allen, 1974.
5. Du Bois, 1930, "Education and Work," Commencement Address at Howard University, June 6. *Journal of Negro Education* 1 (April 1932): 60-74.
6. Karenga, 1982, 221.
7. *Black Panthers: San Francisco State on Strike*, 1998 (VHS), California Newsreel.
8. Quoted in Lewis, 2000, 146. See also R. Cohen, 1977, *When the Old Left Was Young: Student Radicals and America's First Mass Student Movement, 1929-1941.*
9. Coker,(DVD), 2007.
10. Turner, 1980, 83.
11. Ibid.
12. R. Davis, 1943.
13. Turner, 1980.
14. Al-Hadid,.97 in Aldridge and Young, eds., 2000.
15. Gordon,   Ibid., 169.
16. Karenga,   Ibid., 96.
17. Turner, 1980, 56.
18. Ibid., 57.
19. Turner, 1980; Harris, 1982.
20. Harris, 1982, 320.
21. Ibid, 321; Turner, 1980, 58.
22. Allen, 1974; Banks, 1972; Hare, 1969.
23. Blassingame, 1974.

24. Allen, 1974. Arguments are still being waged regarding the appropriateness of politics in Black Studies. See also "A Call to Protect Academic Integrity from Politics," in L.R. and J.A. Gordon, 2006.

25. Turner, 1980.

26. Lange, 1983; Allen, 1974; Banks, 1972; Hare, 1969.

27. Lange, 1983.

28. Allen, 1974; Hare, 1969; Banks, 1972; Turner, 1980; Valentine, 1972.

29. Valentine, 1972, 47.

30. Lange, 1983, 139.

31. Turner, 1980, 59.

32. Genovese, 1969; Wright, 1970.

33. Karenga, 1969; Allen, 1974.

34. Allen, 1974, 6.

35. Banks, 1972.

36. Robinson et.al., 1969.

37. Wilson, 1974.

38. Du Bois, 1898.

39. Davis, 1969.

40. Daniel, 1980; K. Williams, 1981.

41. Karenga, 1969, 38.

42. Wright, 1970; Fischer, 1969; Henshel, 1969.

43. Cruse, 1969, 26.

44. Fischer, 1969.

45. Wright, 1970.

46. Turner, 1980, 21.

47. Blassingame, 1970.

48. Pentony, 1971; Genovese, 1969.

49. Genovese, 1969; Robinson, 1969.

50. Wright, 1970; Blassingame, 1970.

51. Pentony, 1971.

52. Mays, 1974; Hare, 1969; Cruse, 1969; Turner, 1980; Butler, 1981.

53. Butler, 1981.

54. Du Bois, 1935, 328, and in Weinberg, 1970, 190.
55. Long, 1971.
56. Butler, 1981, 8.
57. Cleveland, 1969.
58. R.L. Harris, 1982.
59. Hamilton, 1970.
60. Harris, 1982.
61. Turner, 1980.
62. R.L. Harris, 1982.
63. Ibid., 319.
64. R.L. Harris, 1982.
65. Blassingame, 1970; Turner, 1980; Harris, 1982; Robinson et. Al., 1969.
66. Ford, 1973, 48.
67. Riesman and Jencks, "Colleges: Academic Disaster Areas." 37 *Harvard Educational Review*, (Winter 1967): 3-60.
68. Ford, 1973.
69. Ibid.
70. Ibid., 48.
71. Newton, 1975, 255.
72. Williams, 1981, 30.
73. Du Bois, 1903, 268.
74. Faculty Committee, 1972.
75. http://www.bu.edu/afam/philosophy.html/ (accessed October 2, 2009).
76. Delores P. Aldridge, Grace Towns Hamilton Distinguished Professor of Sociology and African American Studies.
77. Telephone interview with Nathan Huggins, chairperson, Department of Black Studies, Harvard University, August 27, 1984. Today enrollment remains steady.
78. Telephone interview with Adelaide Gulliver, director, Black Studies Center, Boston University, August 27, 1984. Today the program suffers from low enrollment but still offers a master of arts degree.
79. Thelwell, 1969.
80. Wright, 1970.

81. Thelwell, 1969.

82. Robinson et. Al., 1969.

83. Aldridge and Young, 2000, 521-22.

84. Ibid.

85. McWorter, 1969, 55.

86. Kilson, 1969, 30.

87. Wright, 1970; C.H. Taylor, 1969.

88. Mintz, 1969.

89. C.H. Taylor, 1969, 2.

90. Butler, 1981.

91. Newton, 1975.

92. McGeorge Bundy was Ford Foundation president, 1966-1979. *See* Noliwe Rooks, 2007. *White money/black power: The Surprising History of African American Studies and the Crisis of Race in Higher Education,* (Boston: Beacon Press, 2007) for a detailed analysis of the role of white philanthropy in Black Studies.

93. Smith, 1980.

94. Walton, 1974.

95. Robinson et. Al., 1969; Blassingame, 1970.

96. Du Bois, 1903, 215.

97. Ibid., 11.

98. D. Bruce, Jr., "W.E.B. Du Bois and the Idea of Double Consciousness" in Gates and Oliver, 1999, 236; and in 64 *American Literature* (1992):299-309.

99. Young, 2006, 65.

100. Frye, 1976.

101. Butler, 1981, 36.

102. Fischer, 1969.

103. Walton, 1974.

104. Butler 1981; Cruse, 1969; Hare, 1969, 1970; Karenga, 1969; Allen, 1974.

105. Thelwell, 1969, 56.

106. Robinson et. Al., 1969.

107. Jones, 1972.

108. G.T. Marx, 1969.

109. Carmichael and Hamilton, 1967, 5.
110. Wright, 1970, 366.
111. Van den Berghe, 1967.
112. Pentony, 1971.
113. Jones, 1972; G.T. Marx, 1969, 1971; Pettigrew, 1971.
114. Jones, 1972, 154.
115. Glenn, 1965, 105.
116. Ibid.
117. Jones, 1972, 147.
118. Cleaver, 1995, 157-63, in Delgado and Stefancic, eds., 1997.
119. Semmes, 1981.
120. Cole and Gay, 1971.
121. Campbell and Schuman, 1969.
122. Jones, 1972, 172.
123. Hare, 1969, 11.
124. Ibid., 12.
125. Du Bois, 1933, 185.
126. Ibid.
127. Washburn, *Ethnic Studies in the United States* (1981).
128. Du Bois, 1897, 83.
129. Ibid.
130. MSNBC, August 7, 2009.
131. Publication no. 219 (11): 1-23.
132. Ibid.
133. Du Bois, 1900, 257.
134. Du Bois, *Collier's Weekly* (October 20, 1906): 30.
135. Ibid.
136. Du Bois, August 24, 1911, in Lewis, 1995, 47.
137. Du Bois, 1903, 33-75.
138. Ibid.
139. Ibid., 143.
140. Ibid., 1909, 142-58. Quoted in Foner, 1970, 177.
141. Ibid.
142. Ibid., 158.
143. Ibid., in Foner, 1970, 211-17.

144. Ibid., 213-14.
145. No. 31, 62 Congress, 2 Session.
146. Foner, 1970, 226. Also in *Africa in the World Democracy*, New York: NAACP, 28-30.
147. Du Bois 1915, 115 *Atlantic Monthly* 5 (May 1915): 707-714.
148. Ibid., 708.
149. See Welsing, 1991. Theory of Color Confrontation. Psychiatrist Frances Cress Welsing postulates that whites suffer from an inferiority complex because of their inability to produce color.
150. Foner, 1970, 226.
151. Ibid.
152. Du Bois, 1920, 29.
153. Ibid.
154. Du Bois, "Race Pride," 19 *Crisis* (January 1920): 107. Also in Walden, 1972, 262-63.
155. Ibid.
156. Ibid., 263.
157. Du Bois, 1930, "Education and Work." Commencement address at Howard University, June 6, 9 *Bulletin* 5 (January 1931): 1-20. Also in 1 *Journal of Negro History* (April 1932): 60-74.
158. Ibid.
159. Turner in Aldridge and Young, eds., 2000, 70.
160. Lott in Bloom, 2001, 136.
161. *See* Appiah, 87-103, "The Uncompleted Argument: Du Bois and the Illusion of Race," in Bloom 2001; also in 12 *Critical Inquiry* 1 (Autumn 1985).
162. *See also* Lott, "Du Bois on the Invention of Race," 24 *The Philosophical Forum* 1-3 (Fall-Spring 1992-93).
163. Du Bois, 1934. 51 *Crisis* (April-June): 20-21.
164. Du Bois, in Weinberg, 1970, 15.
165. Du Bois, 1911, 21. Also in Lewis, 1995, 76.
166. Du Bois, 1933, 426, in *Crisis* [1980 reprint].
167. Du Bois, 1935, 4 *Journal of Negro Education* (July):328-35. Also in *Fisk News*, 1936.

168. Ibid., 4 *Journal of Negro Education* (July): 333.
169. Ibid., 329.
170. Ibid., 1935, 265-69.
171. Ibid., 69-70.
172. Charles V. Hamilton is one political scientist who argues that Du Bois was a Black Nationalist. *See* Hamilton, 1970.
173. Du Bois, 1940, 319-22.
174. Ibid., 1949, *Midwest Journal* (Winter): 9-11. Quoted in Foner, 1970, 231.
175. Ibid., 11.
176. Ibid., 1960, in Aptheker, 1973.
177. Ibid., 1960, quoted in Provenzo, Jr., 2002, 281.
178. Ibid.
179. Ibid.
180. Aptheker, 1973.
181. Baldwin, [1963] 1984.
182. Aptheker, 1973, 149.
183. Ibid., 150.

CHAPTER 5

1. See Alexander 2001 for an insightful documentation of attitudes toward women beginning with Paul Lawrence Dunbar.
2. Du Bois, 1921 *Darkwater.*
3. James, 1996, 142, "The Profeminist Politics of W.E.B. Du Bois" in *On Race and Culture*, eds. Bell et. Al., eds., 1996, 141-160.
4. Du Bois, 1920. *Darkwater,* 163.
5. Ibid., 165.
6. Ibid., 168.
7. James, in Bell et.al.,eds., 1996, 142.
8. Du Bois, 1921, 172.
9. Ibid., "The Black Mother," *Crisis,* (December 1912): 78.
10. Ibid., 1920, 182.

11. Ibid., 1915, "Woman Suffrage," *Crisis* (month): 29-30.

12. Ibid., 1921, *Darkwater*, 141.

13. Ibid., 1914, 112, "The Philosophy of Mr. Dole," in *The Selected Writings of W.E.B. Du Bois*, W. Wilson and S. Wright, eds., 1970.

14. Du Bois, "Divine Right," 3 *Crisis* 5 (March 1912): 183.

15. Du Bois, 1914, in Wilson, 1970, 278.

16. See Patricia Morton, "The All-Mother Vision of W.E.B. Du Bois," in Morton, *Disfigured Images: The Historical Assault on Afro-American Women* (New York: Praeger, 1991).

17. Giddings, P., *When and Where I Enter: The Impact of Black Women on Race and Sex in America*, (New York: William Morrow, 1984).

18. Aldridge lists racism, sexism, capitalism, and Judeo-Christianity as issues that exacerbate female-male relationships. *See* Focusing: Black Male Female Relationships, (Chicago: Third World Press, 1991).

19. Baraka, quoted in *Gender Talk*, Cole and Guy-Sheftall, eds., 2003, 80.

20. D. Moynihan,"The Negro Family: The Case for National Action," in *Black Matriarchy: Myth or Reality*. Bracey et. Al.(Belmont, CA: Wadsworth, 1971), 150.

21. Hooks, 1981, 9.

22. Walker, 1983, xi.

23. Ntiri, quoted in Hudson-Weems, 2007, 314.

24. Hill Collins, 1996, "What's in a Name?" 26 *Black Scholar* (1): 13.

25. Ibid.

26. *See* Cole and Haniff for an excellent discussion of Afrocentrism and traditionalist paradigms.

27. Hill Collins, 2005, *Black Sexual Politics*, 5.

28. Aldridge, 2007. Quoted in *Contemporary Africana Theory, Thought, and Action*, Hudson-Weems, ed., 2007, 68.

29. Coleman, *Still Brave*, S. James et. Al., eds., 2009, 120.

30. Lemons, 2009, 73.

31. Ibid.

32. Du Bois, 1928, in Lewis, 1995, 130.
33. Ibid.; in Lewis, 1995, 132.
34. That Cullen was gay was common knowledge in Harlem. In "Father of the Bride" Mason Stokes argues that Du Bois must have known as well but may have thought that Cullen could be "cured" of his ailment with the help of "a loving sympathetic wife." *See* in *Next to the Color Line*, Gillman and Weinbaum, eds., 2007, 309.
35. Lewis, 2000, 228.
36. Stokes, in Gillman and Weinbaum, eds., 2007, 289-316.
37. Lewis, 2000, 267.
38. Ibid., 13.
39. Ibid., 381.
40. Du Bois, quoted in Gilkes, "African-American Women, Social Change, and the Sociology of W.E.B. Du Bois" in *W.E.B. Du Bois on Race & Culture*, eds. Bell, et. Al. 1996, 118.
41. Ibid., *Fisk Herald*, 1887, 1888; and in *Creative Writings*, 56-62, 1985. Ed. Aptheker.
42. Ibid., 1921, 154.
43. Gyant, "The Missing Link: Women in Black/Africana Studies," in Aldridge and Young, eds., 2000, 177-89.
44. Hull, P. Bell-Scott, and B. Smith, eds., (New York: The Feminist Press, 1982).
45. M. James, F. Smith Foster, and B. Guy-Sheftall, eds., 2009.
46. Aldridge, 2009, personal communication (October).
47. Ibid., 2007, in *The African American Studies Reader*, Norment, Jr., ed., 204.
48. Ibid., 2000, 197.
49. *See* V. Gordon, 1987, *Black Women, Feminism, and Black Liberation: Which Way?* (Chicago: Third World Press). *See also* "Black Women, Feminism and Black Studies," in *Out of the Revolution*, Aldridge and Young, eds, 2000, 165-75. *See also* Hudson-Weems who offers an essentialist definition of black womanhood in, *Africana Womanism: Reclaiming Ourselves*, (Troy, MI: Bedford Publishing, 1993).

50. Cole and Haniff, 2007, "Building a Home or Black Women's Studies, 1 *Black Women, Gender, Families*, 1 (Spring): 24-45.
51. Ibid., 25.
52. Ibid., 26.
53. Ibid.
54. Ibid.
55. Ibid.,27.
56. Hill Collins, 2009. "When Fighting Words Are Not Enough," in *Still Brave*, S.M. James et.al., eds., 127-153.
57. Christian, 2007, *The African American Studies Reader*, Norment, Jr., ed., 225.
58. Du Bois, 120, 29.
59. Ibid.
60. McCaskill, 2003, ". . . Feminization of Du Bois' Discourse," in *The Souls of Black Folk One Hundred Years Later* Doland Hubbard, ed,. (Columbia, MO: University of Missouri Press).
61. Ibid.,72. There was an argument over the authorship of Brent's book *Incidents in the Life of a Slave Girl* (1861). It was settled when historian Jean Fagan Yellin researched and edited the narrative for republication in 2000.
62. "We Claim Our Rights," in Foner, 1970, 172.
63. Lange, 1983, 146.
64. Du Bois, 1903, in Gates and Oliver, eds., 1999, 90.
65. Lange, 1983.
66. Du Bois, 1968, 170.

REFERENCES

Adams, R.L. 1980. "Evaluating Professionalism in the Context of Afro-American Studies," *Western Journal of Black Studies* 4 (summer): 140–148.

Aldridge, D.P. 2008. *The Educational Thought of W.E.B. Du Bois.* New York: Teachers College Press.

Aldridge, D.P., and C. Young, eds. 2000. *Out of the Revolution.* Lanham, MD: Lexington Books.

Aldridge, D.P., and J. Lincoln, eds. 1984. "Toward a New Role and Function of Black Studies in Historically White and Black Institutions," *Journal of Negro Education* 53: 359–367.

———. 1991. *Focusing: Black Male-Female Relationships.* Chicago: Third World Press.

———. 2007. "Womanist Issues in Black Studies: Toward Integrating African Womanism Into Africana Studies." In *The African American studies Reader,* ed. N. Norment, Jr. Durham: Carolina Academic Press.

———. 2007. *Africana studies: Philosophical perspectives and theoretical paradigms.* Pullman: Washington State University Press.

———. 2007. "Africana Studies and Gender Relations in the Twenty First Century," Aldridge and James eds. In *Africana Studies.* Pullman: Washington State University Press.

Aldridge, D.P., ed. 2008. *Our last hope: Black male-female relationships in change.* Bloomington: Author-House.

Alexander, E. 2001. *Lyrics of Sunshine and Shadow*. New York: Plume.

Alfred, H. 1958. *Toward a Socialist America: A Symposium of Essays.*New York: Peace Publications.

Al-Hadid, A.Y. 2000. "Africana Studies at Tennessee State University: Traditions and Diversity." In Aldridge and Young eds. Lanham, MD: Lexington Books.

Allen, R. 1974. "Politics of the Attack on Black Studies," *The Black Scholar* 1: 6–10.

Allport, G. W. 1954, 1958. *The Nature of Prejudice*. New York: Addison-Wesley.

Anderson, J.D. 1978. "The Hampton Model of Normal School Industrial Education, 1868–1900. *New Perspectives on Black Educational History*. V. Franklin, Ed. Boston: G.K. Hall & Company.

———. 1988. *The Education of Blacks in the South*. Chapel Hill: UNC Press.

Andrews, W. L., ed. 1985. *Critical Essays on W.E.B. Du Bois*. Boston: G.K. Hall & Company.

Appiah, A. 2001. "The Uncompleted Argument: Du Bois and the Illusion of Race. In H. Bloom, ed. *W.E.B. Du Bois*. Philadelphia: Chelsey House.

Aptheker, H., ed. 1973. *The Education of Black People: Ten critiques 1906–1960 by W.E.B. Du Bois*. Amherst: University of Massachusetts.

———. Ed. 1973 and 1978. *The Correspondence of W.E.B. Du Bois*, Vols. 1–3. Amherst: University of Massachusetts Press.

———. Ed. 1973. *An Annotated Bibliography of the Published Writings of W.E.B. Du Bois*. Millwood, New York: Krause.

———. Ed. 1977. *Book Reviews by W.E.B. Du Bois*. Millwood, NY: KTO.

———. Ed. 1985. *Against Racism: Unpublished Essays, Papers, Addresses, 1887- 1961 W.E. B. Du Bois*. Amherst: U of Massachusetts Press.

Asante, M. 1990. *Kemet, Afrocentricity and Knowledge*. New Jersey: Africa World Press.

————. 2007. *An Afrocentric Manifesto*. Malden, MA: Polity Press.

Asante, M., and M. Karenga, eds. 2006. *Handbook of Black Studies*. Thousand Oaks: Sage Publications.

Atlanta University Publications Vols. 1 & 2. 1969. Ed., W. Katz, New York: Arno Press. and the New York Times.

Bailey, T. 1966. *The American Pageant*. Boston: D.C. Heath Publishers.

Baker, H.A. 1993. *Black Studies Rap and the Academy*. Chicago: University of Chicago Press.

Balaji, M. 2007. *The Professor and the Pupil: The Politics of W.E.B. Du Bois and Paul Robeson*. New York: Nations Books.

Baldwin, J. [1955] 1984. *Notes of a Native Son*. Boston: Beacon Press.

————. [1963] 1984 *The Fire Next Time*. Boston: Beacon Press.

Ballard, A.B. [2004]1974. *The Education of Black Folk: The Afro-American Struggle for Knowledge in White America*. New York: Harper & Row.

Banks, J.A. 1972. "Teaching Black Studies for Social Change." *Journal of Afro American Issues*. 1 Fall: 47–54.

Bascom, J. 1881. *Science of Mind*. New York: G.P. Putnam's Sons.

Bauerlein, M. 2004. "Washington, Du Bois and the Black Future." *Wilson Quarterly* 28, no. 4 (September 22): 74–86.

Bell, B., E.R. Grosholz, and J.B. Stewart, eds. 1996. *W.E.B. Du Bois on Race and Culture*. New York: Routledge.

Bergman, P.M. 1969. *The Chronological History of the Negro in America*. New York: Harper & Row Publishers.

Bethune, L. 1969. Afro-American studies: Perspectives toward a definition. *IRCD Bulletin* 51: 9–10.

"Black mood on campus: Symposium." 1969. *Newsweek* , February, 53–9.

Black Panthers: San Francisco State on Strike. 1969. VHS. San Francisco: California Newsreel.

"Black Studies Curricula: University of California, Berkeley. 1969." *Negro History Bulletin* 32: 6.

"Black Studies Vatican: Workshop on the Black World at the Institute of the Black World, Atlanta. 1969." *Newsweek,* August, 74: 38.

Blassingame, J.W. 1970. "Soul or Scholarship: Choices Ahead for Black Studies." *Smithsonian,* 1 (April): 58–65.

———. ed. 1971. *New Perspectives on Black Studies.* Chicago: University of Illinois.

Bloom, H. 2001. *W.E.B. Du Bois.* Philadelphia: Chelsey House.

Blum, E.J., and J.R. Young. 2009. *The Souls of W.E.B. Du Bois: New Essays and Reflections.* Macon, GA: Mercer University Press.

Book Reviews in Scholarly Journals 1886–1974. Arlington, VA: Carrollton Press.

Broderick, F.L. 1958. "The Tragedy of W.E.B. Du Bois." *Progressive* 22 (February): 29–32.

———. 1968. *W.E.B. Du Bois: Negro Leader in a Time of Crisis.* Stanford: Stanford University Press.

Bruce, D. 1996. "W.E.B. Du Bois and the Idea of Double Consciousness." In Bell et.al., eds. *W.E.B. Du Bois on Race and Culture.* New York: Routledge.

Bullock, H. 1970. *A History of Negro Education in the South, From 1619 to the Present.* New York: Praeger Press.

Bundy, M. 1969. *Black Studies in the University.* New Haven: Yale University Press.

Butler, J.E. 1971. *Black studies.* Washington, DC: University Press of America.

Byerman, K.E. 1994. *Seizing the word: History, art, and self in the work of W.E.B. Du Bois.* Athens: University of Georgia Press.

Byrd, R.P., and B. Guy-Sheftall, eds. 2001. *Traps: African American Men on Gender and Sexuality.* Bloomington: Indiana University Press.

Campbell, A., and H. Schuman, 1969. *Racial Attitudes in Fifteen American Cities.* Ann Arbor: Institute for Social Research.

Carmichael, S., and Hamilton, C.V. 1967. *Black power: The Politics of Liberation in America.* New York: Vintage Books.

Carroll, R. 2004. *Saving the Race: Conversations on Du Bois From a Collective Memoir of Souls*. New York: Harlem Moon.

Carvan, S. 1993. *W.E.B. Du Bois and Racial Relations*. Brookfield, CT: Millbrook Press.

Clarke, J.H., E. Jackson, E. Kaiser, and J.H. O'Dell, eds. 1970. *Black Titan: W.E.B. Du Bois*. Boston: Beacon Press.

Cleaver, K. N. [1995] 1997. "The Antidemocratic Power of Whiteness," *Critical White Studies: Looking Behind the Mirror*. R. Delgado and J. Stefancic, eds. Philadelphia: Temple University Press.

Cleveland, B. 1969. "Black Studies in Higher Education." *Phi Delta Kappan* 51 (September): 44–46.

Coker, N. 2007. *Black Studies U.S.A.* DVD documentary.

Cole, J.B. and B. Guy-Sheftall, 2003. *Gender Talk: The Struggle for Women's Equality in African American Communities*. New York: Ballantine Books.

Cole, M. and J. Gay, 1971. "Culture and Memory." *American Anthropology* 7: 554.

Contee, C. 1974. "Henry Sylvester Williams: Pioneer Pan-Africanist." *Black World* 23 (March): 32–37.

Conyers, J.L. Jr., ed. 1997. *Africana Studies: A Disciplinary Quest for Both Theory and Method*. Jefferson, NC: McFarland & Company Publishing.

———, ed 2003. *Afrocentricity and the Academy: Essays on Theory and Practice*. Jefferson, NC: McFarland & Company Publishing.

Cooper, A.J. [1892] 1998. In *The Voice of Anna Julia Cooper*. Eds. Lemert, C. and E. Bhan, Lanham, MD: Rowman & Littlefield Publishers.

Cortada, R.L. 1974. *Black Studies*. Lexington, Massachusetts: Xerox.

Crouch, S. 2002. *Reconsidering The Souls of Black Folk*. Philadelphia: Running Press.

Cruse. H. 1969. "The Integrationist Ethic as a Basis for Scholarly Endeavors." In *Black Studies in the University*. Robinson, et al. eds. 11.

Cumulative Index to Periodical Literature. March 1959, February 1970.

Curl. C.H. 1969. "Black Studies: Form and Content." 13 *CLA Journal* (September):1–9.

Daniel, P.T.K. 1980. "Black Studies: Discipline or Field of Study?" *Western Journal of Black Studies*, 4 (Fall):195–200.

———. 1981. "Theory Building in Black Studies." *The Black Scholar*, 12 (May-June): 29–36.

Davis, D. 1969. "Reflections." In *Black Studies in the University.* Robinson, A.L., D.H. Ogilvie, and C.C. Foster, eds.

Davis F.G. 1941. "The Nature, Scope and Significance of the First *Phylon* Institute. *Phylon.* (Third Quarter): 275–280.

Davis R. 1943. "Data on Negro Life Available at Tuskegee Institute." *Negro College Quarterly,* 1:87–89.

Davis, R.E. 1954. *The American Negro's Dilemma: The Negro's Self-imposed Predicament.* New York: Philosophical Library.

Delgado, R. and J. Stefancic, eds. 1997. *Critical White Studies: Looking Behind the Mirror.* Philadelphia: Temple University Press.

DeMarco, J.P. 1983. *The Social Thought of W.E.B. Du Bois.* Lanham, MD: University Press of America.

Doland, H. ed. 2003. *The Souls of Black Folk One Hundred Years Later.* Columbia: University of Missouri Press.

Douglass, F. 1881. "The Color Line." 132 *North American Review* (7): 295, 567–578.

Drake, St. C. 1979. "What Happened to Black Studies?" *New York University Education Quarterly* 10 (Spring): 9–16.

Du Bois, D.G. 1978. "Du Bois Legacy Under Attack. *Black Scholar* 9 (January): 2–12.

———. 1997. Interviews, Cairo, Egypt. 1988, Cairo, Egypt. 1987, Fisk University.

Du Bois, S.G. 1971. *His Day is Marching On.* New York: Lippincott.

Du Bois, W.E.B. 1897. "The Conservation of Races." *American Negro Academy Occasional Papers*, no. 2. Washington, DC: 5–15. In the Library of Congress, on-line at www.webdubois.org and also on Amazon.com. published by Book Jungle March 14, 2009.; and in *W.E.B. Du Bois on Sociology and the Black Community,* 1978, eds. Green, D.S. and E.D. Driver, in *W.E.B. Du Bois Speaks,* 1970, ed. Foner, P. and in *W.E.B. Du Bois: A Reader* 1995, ed. D.L. Lewis.

———. 1898. "The Negroes of Farmville, Virginia: A Social Study." *United States Bureau of Labor Bulletin,* no. 14. Washington, DC: Government Printing Office.

———. 1898. "The Study of the Negro Problems." *Annals of the American Academy of Political and Social Science.* 11, no.219, 1–23.

———. 1898. Pamphlet. "Careers Open to College-bred Negroes. Two Addresses Delivered by Alumni of Fisk University. In Fisk University Library. Nashville: Fisk University, pp. 1–14.

———. 1899. "The Negro in the Black Belt: Some Social Sketches." *Bulletin of the Department of Labor:* 4. Washington, DC: Government Printing Office.

———. 1899. *The Philadelphia Negro: A Social Study, Together With a Special Report on Domestic Service,* by Isabel Eaton. Philadelphia: University of Pennsylvania Press.

———. 1901. "The Negro Landholder in Georgia." *Bulletin of the Department of* Labor. Washington, DC: Government Printing Office.

———. 1903. *The Souls of Black Folk.* Millwood, New York: Kraus Thomson.

———. 1906. "Letter to department of labor." *The Correspondence of W.E.B. Du Bois vol. 1 1877- 1934.* (ed.) Aptheker, H. Amherst: Univ. of MA Pr. 1973.

_____. 1906. "The Color Line Belts the World," *Collier's Weekly,* (October 20): 30.

———. 1907. "Socialist of the Path." *Horizon* 1 (February):7–8.

———. 1911. *The Quest of the Silver Fleece.* Chicago: A.C. McClurg & Co.

_____. 1912. "I am Resolved," *Crisis* 3 (January): 113.

———. 1919. "What Zionism Means to Jews. *The Crisis* 17 (February):156.

———. 1919. "Pan-African Congress: A Statement." *The Crisis* 40 (November): 7–9.

———. 1919. "Jim Crow." *The Crisis* 17 (January):112–113.

———. 1920. "Marcus Garvey." *The Crisis* 21 (December):58–60.

———. 1921. *Darkwater.* Millwood, New York: Kraus-Thomson.

———. 1921. "To the World." *The Crisis* 22 (November):3–27.

———. 1924. "The Dilemma of the Negro." *American Mercury* 3:34–45.

———. 1932. "Education and Work." *Journal of Negro Education* 1 (April): 60–74.

———. 1933. "The Field and Function of the American Negro College." *Annals of the American Academy of Political and Social Science.* 11, no. 219: 1–23.

———. 1935. "A Negro Nation Within a Nation." *Current History* 62 (June): 265–269.

———. 1936. "Does the Negro Need Separate Schools?" *Fisk News* 6 (June):10. Also in *Journal of Negro Education,* 4, no. 3 (July): 328–335.

———. 1940. *Dusk of Dawn: An Essay Toward an Autobiography of a Race Concept.* New York: Harcourt, Brace.

———. 1942. "Letter to Edwin Embree." In *The Correspondence of W.E.B. Du Bois.* Aptheker, ed. v. II, 1973.

———. 1965. "On the Future of the American Negro." *Freedomways* (First Quarter) (Spring 1965): 117–124.

———. 1952. *In Battle for Peace: The Story of My 83rd Birthday.* New York: Krause Publications.

———. 1957. "Negroes and Socialism." *National Guardian* April 29.

———. 1958. "Socialism." In *Toward a Socialist America. See* Alfred, H., New York: Peace Publications.

———. 1961. "Letter to Communist Party." In *The correspondence of W.E.B. Du Bois. See* Aptheker, 1973.

_____. 1965. 5 *Freedomways* (1) Winter: 117-124.

———. 1968. *The Autobiography of W.E.B. Du Bois.* New York: International.

———. 1970. *The Gift of Black Folk: The Negroes in the Making of America.* New York: Washington Square Press.

————. [1915] 2001. *The Negro*. Philadelphia: University of Pennsylvania Press; (New York: Henry Holt and Co.).

————, ed. [1903] 2003. *The Negro church*. "Introduction" by Phil Zuckerman, Sandra L. Barnes, and Daniel Cady. Lanham, MD: Rowman & Littlefield.

————. 2004. *The Social Theory of W.E.B. Du Bois*. See Zuckerman, P. Thousand Oaks, CA: Pine Forge Press.

————. 2007. *In Battle for Peace: The Story of My 83rd birthday*. New York: Oxford Press.

Du Bois Memorial Park. 1979. Pamphlet. Great Barrington, Massachusetts: National Historical Landmark Publication. A small group of African American Du Bois supporters purchased land in 1969 for the purpose of creating a national memorial. The dedication ceremony took place on October 18, 1969.

Easum, D.B. 1969. "The Call for Black Studies." *Africa Report* 14 (May-June): 16–22.

First three years of the Afro-American Studies Department (The), Harvard University. 1972. Cambridge: Harvard University Press.

Fischer, R.A. 1969. "Ghetto and Gown: The Birth of Black Studies." *Current History* 57:290–300.

Foner, P. 1970. *W.E.B. Du Bois Speaks*, vols. 1 and 2. New York: Pathfinder.

Fontenot, C.J. and M. Morgan, 2001. *W.E.B. Du Bois and Race: Essays Celebrating the Centennial Publication of the Souls of Black Folk*. Macon, GA: Mercer University Press.

Ford, N.A. 1973. *Black Studies: Threat or Challenge*. New York: Krause.

Foster, E.G. 1973. "Carter G. Woodson's *Mis-education of the Negro* Revisited: Black College and Black Studies." *Freedomways* 13 (Winter): 28–38.

Franklin, J.H. 1948. *From Slavery to Freedom*. New York: Alfred A Knopf.

————. 1965. *Three Negro Classics*. New York: Avon.

Franklin, V.P. 2002. "Hidden in Plain View: African American Women, Radical Feminism, and the Origins of Women's

Studies Programs, 1967–1974," *Journal of African American History* 87 (Fall): 433–440.

———. 2003. "Introduction: African American Student Activism in the 20th Century," *Journal of African American History* 88 (Spring): 105–09.

Frye, C. 1976. *The impact of black studies on the curricular of three universities.* Washington, DC: University Press of America.

———. 1977. "Black Studies: Definition and Administrative Model." *Western Journal of Black Studies* (June): 93–97.

———. 1977. "Higher Education in the New Age: The Role of Interdisciplinary Studies." *American Theosophist* (March): 61–64.

———. 1978. *Towards a Philosophy of Black Studies.* San Francisco: R & E Research.

Gates Jr., H.L. and T.H. Oliver, eds. 1999. *The Souls of Black Folk.* New York: Norton.

Genovese, E. 1969. "Black Studies: Trouble Ahead." *Atlantic Monthly.* 222: 37–41.

Gillman, S.K. and A. Weinbaum, 2007. *Next to the Color Line: Gender, Sexuality and W.E.B. Du Bois.* Minneapolis: University of Minnesota Press.

Glenn, N. 1965. "The Role of White Resistance and Facilitation in the Negro Struggle for Equality," *Phylon* 26: 105-116.

Gordon, L.R. and Gordon, J.A. eds. 2006. *A Companion to African-American Studies.* Malden, MA: Blackwell Publishers.

Gordon, V.V. 1981. "The Coming of Age of Black Studies." *Western Journal of Black Studies* 5 (Fall): 231–236.

———. 2000. "Black Women, Feminism, and Black Studies." In Aldridge and Young 2000.

Green, D.S. and E.D. Driver. eds. 1978. *W.E.B. Du Bois On Sociology and the Black Community.* Chicago: University of Chicago Press.

Grossman, J. 1974. "Black Studies in the Department of Labor, 1897–1907." *Monthly Labor Review* 97 (June):17–27.

Guterl, M.P. 2001. *The Color of Race in America.* Cambridge, MA: Harvard University Press.

Guy-Sheftall, B. 1992. "Black Women's Studies: The Interface of Women's Studies and Black Studies." In *The African American Studies Reader*. Ed. N. Norment, Jr.

———, ed. 1995. *Words of Fire: An Anthology of African-American Feminist Thought*. New York: The New Press.

Guy-Sheftall, B. and J. Cole. 2003. *Gender Talk: The Struggle for Women's Equality in African American Communities*. New York: Ballantine Books.

Gyant, L. 2000. "The Missing Link: Women in Black/Africana Studies." In *Out of the Revolution*. See Aldridge & Young.

Hall, Raymond L., ed. 1977. *Black separatism and social reality: rhetoric and reason*. New York: Pergamon Press.

Hamilton, C.V. 1970. "The Question of Black Studies." *Phi Delta Kappan* 51 (March): 365–368.

Harding, V. 1980. *The Other American Revolution*. Atlanta: Institute of the Black World.

Hare, N. 1969. "What Should be the Role of Afro-American Education in the Undergraduate Curriculum." *Liberal Education* (March) 55:42–50.

———. 1970. "What Black Studies Mean to Black Scholars." *College University Business* 48 (May):56–60.

———. 1972. "The Struggle of Black Students." *The Journal of Afro-American Issues* 1 (Fall): 22.

Harlen, L.H. 1972. *Booker T. Washington: The Making of a Black Leader 1856–1901*. New York : Oxford University Press.

———. 1983. *Booker T. Washington: The Wizard of Tuskegee, 1901–1915*. New York: Oxford University Press.

Harris, J., and G. Davis, 1974. *Black Studies: A Challenge to the American Education System*. Amherst: University of Massachusetts.

Harris, R.L. 1982. "Segregation and Scholarship: The American Council of Learned Societies' Committee on Negro Studies, 1941–1950." *Journal of Black Studies* 12 (March): 315–331.

Harris, T.E. 1993. *Analysis of the Clash Over the Issues Between Booker T. Washington and W.E.B. Du Bois*. New York: Garland.

Hatch, J. 1969. "Black Studies: The Real Issue." *Nation* 108 (June 16): 755–58.

Hector, M.G. 1979. *Racism, Black Nationalism and W.E.B. Du Bois: A Study of a Divided Soul.* Ph.D. diss. Emory University.

Henshel, A.M., and R.L. Henshel, 1969. "Black Studies Programs: Promise and Pitfalls." *Journal of Negro Education.* 38 (Fall): 423–429.

Herskovits, M. 1941. *The Myth of the Negro Past.* New York: Harper.

———. 1966. *The New World Negro.* Bloomington, Indiana: Indiana University Press.

Hill Collins, P. 2000. *Black Feminist Thought: Knowledge, Consciousness, and the Politics of Empowerment.* New York: Routledge.

———. 2001. "What's in a Name? Womanism, Black Feminism, and Beyond," 26 *The Black Scholar* (1): 9–16.

———. 2005. *Black Sexual Politics: African Americans, Gender, and the New Racism.* New York: Routledge.

Hooks, B. 1981. *Ain't I a Woman: Black Women and Feminism.* Boston: South End Press.

———. 1984. *Feminist Theory From Margin to Center.* Boston: South End Press.

———. 2009. "Black Women Shaping Feminist Theory." In *Still Brave. See* James, Foster, and Guy-Sheftall 2009.

Horne, G. 1986. *Black and Red: W.E.B. Du Bois and the Afro-American Response to the Cold War, 1944–1963.* Albany, NY: State University of New York Press.

Hubbard, D. 2003. *The Souls of Black Folk One Hundred Years Later.* Columbia, MO: University if Missouri Press, 2003.

Hudson-Weems, C. 2007. *Contemporary Africana Theory Thought and Action: A Guide to Africana Studies.* Trenton, NJ: Africa World Press.

———. 2007. *Nommo/Self-naming, Self-defining, and the History of Africana Womanism.* Trenton, NJ: Africa World Press.

Hurston, Z.N. 1935. *Mules and Men.* New York: Lippincott.

Ikemma, W.N. 1975. "Another Side of the Black Studies Debacle." *Black Political Economy* 5 (Spring):284–287.

Index to Book Reviews in Humanities Journals 1802–1974. Woodbridge, Ct.: Research Publications.

International Encyclopedia. 1967 ed. s.v. "Abyssinia."

James, C.B. 2009. *Garvey, Garveyism and the Antinomies in Black Redemption.* Trenton, NJ: Africa World Press.

James, J. 1996. "The Profeminist Politics of W.E.B. Du Bois With Respect to Anna Julia Cooper and Ida B. Wells Barnett" in *W.E.B. Du Bois on Race and Culture. See* Bell, B., E. Grosholz, and J. Stewart. New York: Routledge.

James, S.M., F. S. Foster, and B. Guy-Sheftall, eds. 2009. *Still Brave: The Evolution of Black Women's Studies.* New York: The Feminist Press.

Johnson, B. 2008. *W.E.B. Du Bois: Toward Agnosticism.* Lanham, MD: Rowan & Littlefield.

Johnson, K., and E. Watson, 2004. "The W.E.B. Du Bois and Booker T. Washington Debate: Effects Upon African American Roles in Engineering and Engineering Technology." *Journal of Technology Studies.* 30l, no. 4 (Fall): 65–70.

Jones, J.M. 1972. *Prejudice and Racism.* Reading, Mass.: Addison-Wesley.

———. 1996. *Prejudice and Racism.* New York: McGraw-Hill.

Jordan, W. 1968. *White Over Black.* Chapel Hill: University of North Carolina Press.

———.1974. *The White Man's Burden.* London: Oxford University Press.

Kaplan, S. 1982. "Towards a More Creative Scholarship." *Integrated Education* 20 (May-Oct): 3–5.

Karenga, M. 1982. *Introduction to Black Studies.* Los Angeles: University of Sankore Press.

Karenga, M. 1969. "The Black Community and the University." *Black Studies in the University.* New Haven: Yale.

Keller, M. and C.J. Fontenot, Jr., ed. 2007. *Re-Cognizing W.E.B. Du Bois in the Twenty-first Century.* Macon, GA: Mercer University Press.

Kelley, R. and E. Lewis, eds. 2000. *To Make Our World Anew.* New York: Oxford University Press.

Kendhammer, B. 2007. "Du Bois the Pan-Africanist and the Development of African Nationalism." *Ethnic & Racial Studies.* 30 January 1: 51–71.

Kilson, M. 1969. "Black Studies Movement: A Plea for Perspective." *Crisis* 76 (October): 327.

King, G.D. 1983. "Black Studies: An Idea in Crisis." *Western Journal of Black Studies* 6 (Winter): 241–245.

Kirschke, A.H. 2007. *Art in Crisis: W.E.B. Du Bois and the Struggle for African American Identity and Memory.* Bloomington: Indiana University Press.

Knowles, L.L., and K. Prewitt, eds., 1969. *Institutional Racism in America.* Englewood Cliffs, N.J.: Prentice-Hall.

Lacy, L. 1970. *Cheer the Lonesome Traveler.* New York: Dial.

Lange, W.J. 1983. "W.E.B. Du Bois and the First Scientific Study of Afro-American." *Phylon.* 44 (June): 135–146.

Law, R. 2007. "Du Bois as a Pioneer of African History: A Reassessment of *The Negro* 1915." In *Recognizing W.E.B. Du Bois in the Twenty-first Century.* Keller M. and C. Fontenot, Jr. eds. Macon, GA: Mercer University Press.

Laws, J.B. 1902. "The Negro of Cinclare Central Factory and Calumet Plantation, Louisiana." *Bulletin of the Department of Labor,* 7.

Lawson, F. and M. Merrill, 1984. *The Three Sarahs: The Woman Question in African American Public Culture 1830–1900.* New York: Edwin Mellen Press.

Lemons, G.L. 2001. "When and Where [We] Enter": In search of a feminist forefather, reclaiming the womanist legacy of W.E.B. Du Bois." In *Traps See* Byrd and Guy-Sheftall.

Lemons, G.L. 2009. *Womanist Forefathers: Frederick Douglass and W.E.B. Du Bois.* New York: SUNY Press.

Lester, J. 1971. *The Seventh Son: The Thoughts and Writings of W.E.B. Du Bois.* New York: Random House.

Levine, L. 1977. *Black Culture and Black Consciousness: Afro-American Folk Thought From Slavery to Freedom.* New York: Oxford University Press.

Lewis, D.L. 1993. *W.E.B. Du Bois: The Biography of a Race 1868–1919*. New York: Henry Holt.

———. ed. 1995. *W.E.B. Du Bois a Reader*. New York: Henry Holt.

———. 2000. *W.E.B. Du Bois: The fight for Equality and the American century 1919–1963*. New York: Henry Holt.

Long, R.A. 1971. "Black Studies Year One." *Report, Atlanta University Center for African and African-American Studies*. Atlanta: Atlanta University. N.p.

———. 1977. "Black Studies: Year One." In *Black Separatism and Social Reality: Rhetoric and Reason*. R.L. Hall, ed. New York: Pergamon Press.

Marable, M. 1986. *W.E.B. Du Bois: Black Radical Democrat*. Boston: Twayne Publishers.

———. 1998. *Black Leadership*. New York: Columbia University Press.

Marx, G.T. 1969. *Protest and Prejudice: A Study of Belief in the Black Community*. New York: Harper & Row.

Mayo, A. 1942. "Charles Lewis Reason." In *Negro History Bulletin* 5 June 212–215.

Mays, B.E. 1974. "Black Colleges: Past, Present and Future." *Black Scholar* 6 (September): 32–36.

McClendon, W.H. 1974. "Black studies: Education for Liberation." *Black Scholar* 6 (September): 54.

McGill, R. 1965. "W.E.B. Du Bois," *The Atlantic Monthly.*216 (5) 78–81.

McWorter, G. 1969. "Deck the Ivy Racist Halls: The Case for Black Studies." In *Black Studies in the University. see.* Robinson, et al.

———. 1981. *The Professionalization of Achievement in Black Studies*. Chicago: The Center for Afro-American Studies.

Mintz, S.W. 1969. *Black Studies in the University*. New Haven: Yale.

Mocombe, P.C. 2009. *The Soul-less Souls of Black Folk*. Lanham, MD.: University Press of America.

Montagu, A. 1945. *Man's Most Dangerous Myth: The Fallacy of Race*. New York: Columbia University Press.

Moon, H.L. 1972. *The Emerging Thought of W.E.B. Du Bois.* New York: Simon & Schuster.

Moore, J. 2003. *Booker T. Washington, W.E.B. Du Bois, and the Struggle for Racial Uplift.* Wilmington, Delaware: SR Books.

Mootry, M.K. 1983. "J. Saunders Redding: A Case Study of the Black Intellectual." *Western Journal of Black Studies* 7 (Summer): 62–67.

Morais, H. 1967. *The History of the Negro in Medicine.* New York: Johnson Publishers.

Moses, W.J. 2004. *Creative Conflict in African American Thought: Frederick Douglass, Alexander Crummell, Booker T. Washington, W.E.B. Du Bois, and Marcus Garvey.* Cambridge: University of Cambridge Press.

Newton, J.E. 1975. "A Review of Black Studies as Related to Basic Elements of Curriculum." *Afro-American Studies* 3: 255.

Norment, N. 2001. *African American Studies Reader.* Durham, NC: Carolina Academic Press.

Ntiri, D.W. 2007. "Africana Womanism: The Coming of Age." In *Contemporary Africana Theory Thought and Action. See* Hudson-Weems, 2007.

Pentony, J. 1971. "The Case for Black Studies." In *New Perspectives on Black Studies. See* Blassingame, Chicago: University of Chicago.

Peterson, C. 2007. *Du Bois, Fanon, Cabral: The Margins of Elite Anti-colonial Leadership.* Lanham, MD: Lexington Books.

Pettigrew, T.F. 1971. *Racially Separate or Together.* New York: Mc Graw Hill.

Provenzo Jr., E. ed., 2002. *Du Bois on Education.* New York: Rowman & Littlefield Publishers.

Rabaka, R. 2007. *W.E.B. Du Bois and the Problems of the Twenty-first Century: An Essay on Africana Critical Theory.* Lanham, MD: Lexington Books.

Rampersad, A. [1976] 1990. *The Art and Imagination of W.E.B. Du Bois.* New York: Schocken Books.

Randall, D. [1952] 1967. *Booker T. and W.E.B.* Detroit: Broadside Press.

Redkey, E. 1969. "On Teaching and Learning Black History." In *Black Studies in the University.* See Robinson, et al.

Reed, A.L. 1997. *W.E.B. Du Bois and American Political Thought: Fabinism and the Color Line.* New York: Oxford University Press.

Richards, H.J. ed., 1971. *Topics in Afro-American Studies.* New York: Black Academy Press.

Roberts, S.V. 1970. "Black Studies: More Than Soul Courses." *Commonwealth* 51 (January 30): 478–79.

Robinson, A.L., C.C. Foster, and D.H. Ogilvie, eds., 1969. *Black Studies in the University.* New Haven: Yale University Press.

Rojas, F. 2007. *From Black Power to Black Studies.* Baltimore: Johns Hopkins University Press.

Rooks, N. 2007. *White Money/Black Power.* Boston: Beacon Press.

Rose, A.W. 1975. *Afro-American Studies in Higher Education.* Miami: University of Miami.

Rosovsky, H. 1969. "Black Studies at Harvard: Personal Reflections Concerning Recent Events." *American Scholar*, 38 (Autumn): 562–572.

Rosser, J.M. 1972. "Higher Education and the Black American: An overview." *The Journal of Afro-American Issues*, 1 (Fall): 22.

Rucker, W. 2002. "A Negro Nation Within a Nation: W.E.B. Du Bois and the Creation of a Revolutionary Pan-Africanist Tradition, 1903–1947." 32 *Black Scholar*, no. 3/4 (2002): 37.

Rudwick, E. [1960] 1982. *W.E.B. Du Bois: Voice of the Black Protest Movement.* Urbana: University of Illinois Press.

——— 1960. *W.E.B. Du Bois: A Study in Minority Group Leadership.* Philadelphia: University of Pennsylvania.

Rustin, B. 1969. *Black Studies: Myths and Realities.* New York: Harper.

Semmes, C. 1981. "Foundations of an Afrocentric Social Science, Implications for Curriculum-building, Theory, and Research." *Journal of Black Studies* 12 (September): 3–17.

———. 1982. "Black Studies and the Symbolic Structure of Domination." *Western Journal of Black Studies* 6 (Summer):116–122.

Smith, W.D., and A.C. Yates, 1980. "Editorial in Black Studies." *Journal of Black Studies* 10 (March): 269–277.

Standing Committee to Develop the Afro-American Studies Department: A Progress Report 1969. Cambridge: Harvard University Press.

Stokes, M. 2007. "Father of the Bride." In *Next to the Color Line: Gender, sexuality, and W.E.B. Dubois. See* Gillman, S. and A.R. Weinbaum.

Sutton, W.S. 1972. *The Evolution of the Black Studies Movement.* Dayton: Ohio University Press.

Taylor, C.H. 1969. "Preface." In *Black Studies in the University. See* Robinson, et al. New Haven: Yale University Press.

Taylor, C.M. 1981. "W.E.B. Du Bois' Challenge to Scientific Racism." *Journal of Black Studies* 11 (June):449–460.

Thelwell, M. 1969. "Black Studies: A Political Perspective." In *Black Studies, See* Butler. 1981. Washington, DC: University Press of America.

Thom, W.T. 1901. "The Negroes of Litwalton, Virginia; A Social Study of the Oyster Negro." *United States Bureau of Labor Bulletin.* 14.

Turner, J. 1980. "Black Studies as an Integral Tradition in African-American Intellectual History." *The Journal of Negro Education* 49:52–59.

Valentine, C.A. 1972. *Black Studies and Anthropology.* Philippines: Addison-Wesley.

van den Berghe, P. 1967. *Race and Racism: A Comparative Perspective.* New York: Wiley.

Von Eschen, P. 1997. *Race Against Empire: Black Americans and Anti Colonialism 1937–1957.* Ithaca: Cornell University Press.

Vontress, C.E. 1970. "Black Studies—Boon or Bane?" *Journal of Negro Education* 39 (Summer):192–201.

Walden, D. 1972. *W.E.B. Du Bois: The Crisis Writings.* Greenwich, CT: Fawcett Books.

Walker, A. 1983. *In Search of Our Mother's Gardens*. New York: Harcourt Brace Jovanovich.

Walters, R., R.C. Smith, 1979. "The Black Education Strategy in the 1970s." *Journal of Negro Education* 48 (Spring):156–170.

Walton, S.F. 1974. "Black Studies and Affirmative Action." *The Black Scholar* 6 (September): 71.

Warren, N. 1984. The Contributions of W.E.B. Du Bois to Black Studies in Higher Education. Ph.D. diss., University of Mississippi.

Washburn, D.E. 1981. *Ethnic Studies in the United States: Higher Education*. Washington, DC: Office of Education.

Washington, B.T. 1901. *Up From Slavery*. New York: Pathfinder.

———. (1896) "The Awakening." Np. Retrieved May 1, 2009, from www.Atlantic.com/

W.E.B. Du Bois of Great Barrington. 1992. Videorecording. Alexandria, VA: PBS.

W.E.B. Du Bois: A Biography in Four Voices. 1995. Videorecording. San Francisco: California Newsreel.

Weinberg, M. ed., 1970. *W.E.B. Du Bois: A Reader*. New York: Harper & Row.

Wells, H. G. 1971. *The Outline of History*. Garden City: Doubleday.

Welsch, E.K. 1965. *The Negro in the United States: A Research Guide*. Bloomington: Indiana University.

Welsing, F.C. 1991. *The Isis Papers: The Keys to the Colors*. Chicago: Third World Press.

West, Cornel. 1999. *The Cornel West Reader*. New York: Basic Civitas Books.

Whitten, N.E., J.F. Szwed, 1970. *Afro-American Anthropology: Contemporary Perspectives*. New York: Macmillian Publishers.

Wilcox, P. 1970. Black Studies as an Academic Discipline. *Negro Digest* 19 (March):75–87.

Williams, D.G. *Ethnicity and Cultural Authority From Arnold to Du Bois*. 2006. Edinburgh: University of Edinburgh.

Williams, K. 1981. "Down By One is Still Losing: The Black Studies Syndrome." *Change* 13 (October):30–37.

Willie, C.U., R. Edmonds, 1978. *Black Colleges in America: Challenge, Development Survival.* New York: Teacher's College.

Wilson, C.E. 1969. "Case for Black Studies." *Education Leadership* 27 (December): 218–221.

Wilson, R. 1974. "Responses of Sociologists to Black Studies." In *Black Sociologists: Historical and Contemporary Perspectives.* Eds. Blackwell, J. and M. Janowitz. Chicago: University of Chicago Press.

Wilson, W. S.J. Wright, eds., 1970. *The Selected Writings of W.E.B. Du Bois.* New York: New American Library.

Wilson, W.J. 1978. *The Declining Significance of Race: Blacks and Changing American Institutions.* Chicago: University of Chicago.

Wiltse, C. ed., 1965. *David Walker's Appeal.* New York: Hill & Wang.

Winston, M. 1971. "Through the Back Door: Academic Racism and the Negro Scholar in Historical Perspective." *Daedalus* 100:678–719.

Wolfenstein, E.V. 2007. *A Gift of the Spirit: Reading the Souls of Black folk.* Ithaca: Cornell University Press.

Wolters, R. 2002. *Du Bois and His Rivals.* Columbia: University of Missouri Press.

————. 1975. *The New Negro on Campus:Black College Rebellions of the 1920s.* Princeton, NJ: Princeton University Press.

Wright, S.J. 1970. "Black Studies and Sound Scholarship." *Phi Delta Kappan* 51 (March): 365–68.

Young, A.A. et al., eds., 2006. *The Souls of W.E.B. Du Bois.* Boulder: Paradigm Publishers.

Zackodnik, T. ed., 2007. *African American Feminisms 1828–1923.* New York: Routledge.

Zamir, S. 1995. *Dark voices: W.E.B. Du Bois and American Thought, 1888–1903.* Chicago: University of Chicago Press.

Zhang, J. 2001. *W.E.B. Du Bois: The Quest for Abolition of the Color Line.* New York: Routledge.

Zuckerman, P. ed., 2004. *The Social Theory of W.E.B. Du Bois.* Thousand Oaks, CA: Pine Forge Press.

SELECTED BIBLIOGRAPHY

Adams, J.M. 1905. "Rough Sketches: W.E. Burghardt Du Bois, Ph.D." In *The Voice of the Negro*. 2 (March):175–181.

Adams, R.L. 1980. "Evaluating Professionalism in the Context of Afro-American Studies." *Western Journal of Black Studies* 4 (Summer):140–48.

Alkalimat, A. 2003. "A 21st Century Challenge." www.eblack-studies.org/eblack.html/ (accessed September 28, 2009).

Allen, H.S. 1971. "William Edward Burghardt Du Bois." *Great Black Americans*. West Haven: Pendulum.

Allen, R.L. 1975. *Reluctant Reformers: Racism and Social Reform Movements in the United States*. Garden City, New York: Anchor.

Aptheker, H. 1948. "W.E.B. Du Bois: The First Eighty Years." *Phylon*. (First Quarter) 9:59–62.

———. 1949. "The Washington-Du Bois Conference of 1904." *Science and Society* 13:344–351.

———. 1950. "W.E.B. Du Bois: Story of a half century of distinguished service to humanity." *National Guardian* February 8: 6–7.

———. 1962. *A Documentary History of the Negro People in the United States*. New York: The Citadel Press.

———. 1965. "Some Unpublished Writings of W.E.B. Du Bois." *Freedomways* 5 (Winter): 103–128.

———. 1973. *Afro-American History, The Modern Era*. Secaucus, NJ: Citadel Press.

Bailey, R.W., and G.A. Mc Worter, eds., 1980. *Black Studies Curriculum Development in the Eighties; Pattern of Consensus, Conflict, and Change.* Urbana, IL: University of Illinois Press.

Baker, R.S. 1964. *Following the Color Line.* New York: Harper & Row.

Baldwin, J. [1963] 1964. *The Fire Next Time.* New York: Mass Market Paperback.

Bardolph, R. ed., 1970. *The Civil Rights Record: Black Americans and the Law 1849–1977.* New York: Thomas Crowell .

Bell, D. 1977. "The Legacy of W.E.B. Du Bois: A Rational Model for Achieving Public School Equity for America's Black Children." *Creighton Law Review* (December.) 409.

Bennett, L. 1975. *The Shaping of Black America.* Chicago: Johnson Publishers.

Bergman, P.M. 1969. *The Chronological History of the Negro in America.* New York: Harper & Row.

Boggs, J. 1970. *Racism and the Class Struggle: Further Pages from a Black Worker's Notebook.* New York: Modern Reader.

Bond, H. M. 1934. *The Education of the Negro in the American Social Order.* Englewood Cliffs, NJ: Prentice-Hall.

———. 1939. *Negro Education in Alabama: A Study in Cotton and Steel.* Washington, DC: Associated Publishers.

Bontemps, A. 1961. *One Hundred Years of Negro Freedom.* New York: Dodd, Mead.

Braithwaite, W.S. 1940. "A tribute to W.E. Burghardt Du Bois." *Phylon.* 10: 302–306.

Breathett, G. 1975. "William Edward Burghardt Du Bois: An Address to the Academic Community." *Journal of Negro History* 60 (January):45–52.

Brimmer, A. 1969. "The Black Revolution and the Economic Future of Negroes in the United States." *American Scholar* 38 (Autumn):629–43.

Broderick, F.L. 1958. "German Influence on the Scholarship of W.E.B. Du Bois." *Phylon* 19 (December):367–371.

———. 1958. "The Academic Training of W.E.B. Du Bois." *Journal of Negro Education* 27 (Winter):10–16.

————. 1959. *W.E.B. Du Bois, Negro Leader in a Time of Crisis.* Stanford: Stanford University Press.

————, et al. 1965. *Negro Protest Thought in the Twentieth Century.* Indianapolis, IN: Bobbs Merrill.

Bullock, H.A. 1967. *A History of Negro Education in the South From 1619 to the Present.* Cambridge: Harvard University Press.

Bunzell, J.H. 1968. Black Studies at San Francisco State. *Public Interest,* (Fall): 22–38.

Burns, H. 1970. "The Washington Du Bois Controversy." *Afro-American Studies* 1: 51–50.

Butler, J.E. 1979. "Black Studies and Sensibility: Identity, the Foundation for a Pedagogy." *Western Journal of Black Studies* 3:290–93.

Carnoy, M. 1974. *Education as Cultural Imperialism.* New York: David McKay.

Cash, W.J. 1941. *The Mind of the South.* New York: Random House.

Chew, P. 1970. "Black History, or Black Mythology?" *American Heritage* 20 (August): 4–9.

Clark, J.H. 1974. *Marcus Garvey and the Vision of Africa.* NY: Vintage Books.

Cleaver, E. 1969. "Education and Revolution." *Black Scholar* 1 (November): 44–52.

Cohen, S. 1974. *Education in the United States: A Documentary History.* New York: Random House.

Cole, J. B. 1970. "Culture: Negro, Black and Nigger." *Black Scholar* 1:40–44.

————. 1981. "Black women as colleagues in black studies." *New England Journal of Black Studies* pp. 3–8.

Contee, C.G. 1969. The Emergence of Du Bois as an African Nationalist. *Journal of Negro Education* 54 (January): 48–63.

————. 1972. "Du Bois, the NAACP, and the Pan-African Congress of 1919." *Journal of Negro History* (January) 57.

Cruse, H. 1967. *The Crisis of the Negro Intellectual.* New York: Wm. Marrow.

————. 1968. *Rebellion or Revolution*. New York: Wm. Morrow.

Dillon, M.L. 1970. "White Faces and Black Studies." 30 *Commonwealth* (January): 476–479.

Drimmer, M. 1970. "Teaching Black History in America: What are the Problems?" *Negro History Bulletin* 33 (February): 32–34.

Du Bois, W.E.B. 1894. *A Rational System of Negro Education*. Ms. Du Bois Papers. Fisk University Library, Nashville, TN.

Franklin, J.H. 1956. *The Militant South*. Cambridge: Harvard University.

Franklin, V.P. and J.D. Anderson, eds., 1978. *New Perspectives on Black Educational History*. Boston: G.K. Hall.

Freire, P. 1968. *Pedagogy of the Oppressed*. New York: Seabury.

Garvey, A.J. 1970. *Garvey and Garveyism*. New York: Macmillan.

————. 1977. *Philosophy and Opinions of Marcus Garvey*. New York: Atheneum.

Gibson, E.F. 1979. "Three D's: Distortion, Deletion, Denial." *Social Education* 33 (April): 405–409.

Glenn, N. 1965. "The Role of White Resistance and Facilitation in the Negro Struggle for Equality." *Phylon* 26:105–116.

Green, D.S. 1975. "W.E.B. Du Bois Memorial Park." *Freedomways* 15:258–264.

Hall, R.L. ed., 1977. *Black Separatism and Social Reality: Rhetoric and Reason*. New York: Pergamon Press.

Harding, V. 1969. "Achieving Educational Equality: Stemming the Black Brain Drain." *Current* CV (March): 37–40.

————. 1969. "Black Students and the 'Impossible' Revolution." *Ebony* 24 (August): 141–149.

Henderson, L. J. 1970. "W.E.B. Du Bois: Black Scholar and Prophet." *Black Scholar* (January-February): 48–57.

Herskovits, M.J. 1941. "The Interdisciplinary Aspects of Negro Studies." *American Council of Learned Societies Bulletin*. 32–39.

————. 1946. "Problem Method and Theory in Afroamerican Studies." *Phylon*: 337–354.

————. 1948. "The Contribution of Afroamerican Studies to Africanist Research." *American Anthropologist.* 50:1–10.

————. 1951. "The Present Status and Needs of Afroamerican Research." *Journal of Negro History.* 36:123–147.

Hofstadter, R. 1955. *Social Darwinism in American Thought.* New York: Brazille.

Huggins, N.I., and M. Kilson, eds., 1974. *Key Issues in Afro-American Experiences.* New York: Harcourt Brace & Jovanovich.

Jackson, G.G. 1982. "Black Psychology an Avenue to the Study of Afro-Americans." *Journal of Black Studies* 12 (March): 241–260.

Jones, R. 1996. "Black Studies Comes to Power." *Black Issues in Higher Education* (December 26): 80–83.

Knowles, L.L., Prewitt, K. 1969. *Institutional Racism.* Englewood Cliffs, NJ: Prentice-Hall.

Knox, E.O. 1933. "The Negro as a Subject of University Research in (1932–1951)." *Journal of Negro Education* (Fall) 21:36.

Kovel, J. 1970. *White Racism: A Psychological History.* New York: Pantheon.

Meier, A. 1964. *Negro Thought in America 1880–1915.* Ann Arbor: University of Michigan Press.

Memmi, A., 1967. *The Colonizer and the Colonized.* Boston: Beacon Press.

Miller, K. 1968. *Radicals and Conservatives and Other Essays on the Negro in America.* New York: Schocken Books.

Milne, E. 1984. "Black Studies Today." *Essence* 14 (April): 26–27.

Moses, W.J. 1978. *The Golden Age of Black Nationalism 1850–1925.* Hamden, CT: Anchor.

Myrdal, G. 1944. *An American Dilemma: The Negro Problem and Modern Democracy.* New York: Harper.

Paschal, A.G. 1971. "The Spirit of W.E.B. Du Bois." *Black Scholar* 2 (February): 19.

Poinsett, A. 1970. "Think Tank for Black Scholars." 35 *Ebony* (February): 46–48.

Redding, J.S. l949. "Portrait: W.E. Burghardt Du Bois." *American Scholar* 62 (January): 44–56.

Redding, S. 1969. "The Black Youth Movement." *American Scholar* 28 (Autumn): 584–587.

Rist, R. 1970. "Black Staff, Black Studies and White Universities: A Study in Contradictions." *Journal of Higher Education* 41 (November): 618–629.

Rousseve, R.J. 1969. "Dealing Responsibly With the Black Americans." *Negro Educational Review* 20 (October): 95–105.

Rudwick, E.M. 1968. *W.E.B. Du Bois: Propagandist of Negro Protest.* New York: Atheneum Press.

Social Science Institute. 1946. *Racial Attitudes, Social Science Source Document no. 3.* Nashville, TN.: Social Science Institute of Fisk Univ.

"Student Strikes: 1968–69." 1970. *Black Scholar* 1 (January-February): 65–75.

Stumpter, R.D. 1973. A Critical Study of the Educational Thought of W.E.B. Du Bois. Ph.D., diss., George Peabody College of Vanderbilt University.

Tuttle, W.M. ed., 1973. *W.E.B. Du Bois.* Englewood Cliffs, NJ: Prentice-Hall.

———. 1974. "W.E.B. Du Bois, Confrontation With White Liberalism During the Progressive Era: A *Phylon* document." 35 *Phylon* (September):19–37.

Walden, D., ed., 1972. *W.E.B. Du Bois: The Crisis writings.* Greenwich, CT: Fawcett.

Wicker, A.W. 1969. "Attitudes Versus Actions: The Relationship of Verbal and Covert Behavior Responses to Attitude Objects." 25 *Journal of Social Issues*: 41–78.

Wolters, R. 1975. *The New Negro on Campus: Black College Rebellions of the 1920s.* Princeton: Princeton University Press.

Woodson, C. G. 1933. *The Mis-education of the Negro.* Washington, D.C.: Associated Publications.

———. 1968. *The Education of the Negro Prior to 1861.* New York: Arno Press and the New York Times.

Woodward, C.V. 1974. *The Strange Career of Jim Crow.* New York: Oxford University.

Wright, W.D. 1978. "Du Bois' Theory of Political Democracy." *The Crisis* 85:85–89.

INDEX

Covey, Steven, 31
"Credo," 138, 157
Cruickshank, U.S. v., 8
Crummell, Alexander, 30
Cruse, H., 111, 115
Cullen, Countee, 177-178
"Cult of True Womanhood,"
175
"culturally deprived" thesis, 113
cultural pluralism, 111, 133
culture: Black, 82; European,
21–25; not defined by Du
Bois, 24
Curry, J.L.M., 36

"The Damnation of Women,"
166-167
Darkwater, 142, 143, 157, 186
Daughters of Rebecca, 73
"daughters of sorrow," 167
Delaney, Martin R., 39, 134
Department of Labor Reports,
xxi, 62, 103
Dill, Augustus, 78
discrimination, mother's
belief about, 5
Disraeli, Benjamin, 6, 7
"Does the Negro Need Sepa-
rate Schools?" 87, 113, 148
double consciousness, xix,
123, 124, 128, 142
Douglass, Frederick, 7, 24,
35, 61, 165, 170, 176
Drake, St. Clair, 102
Dred Scott decision, 7

Du Bois, David Graham, xxi,
54
Du Bois, Mary Silvina
(Burghardt), 1, 11
Du Bois, Nina (Gomer), 166,
177, 179
Du Bois, Shirley (Graham),
xx, 55, 179
Du Bois, W.E.B.: biographical, 1-5; Black Studies,
contributions to, 61-99,
153-63; as citizen of Ghana,
59; and communism, 56-59;
critical of U.S. Govern-
ment, 50–53; death, 60;
disagreement with Wash-
ington, 27-37; family, 177-
179; joined Socialist Party,
46; racial identity, 12-13;
as reporter/editor, 180;
self-identity, 12; teacher at
Wilberforce University, 24;
as teacher in Tennessee, 13;
teaching at Atlanta University, 26; and U.S. government, 50–53; (William
Edward Burghardt), xvi,
2; works, currently over-
looked, 186-189; world
travel (1958–1959), 55-56;
writings (1896–1910), xix
Du Bois, Yolande, 166,
177-179
Du Bois–Garvey dispute, 41-44
Dunn, Oscar J., 7
Dusk of Dawn, 33, 150, 157